I0427872

Highway/Marine Accident Report

U.S. Towboat *Robert Y. Love*
Allision With Interstate 40 Highway Bridge
Near Webbers Falls, Oklahoma
May 26, 2002

NTSB/HAR-04/05
PB2004-916205
Notation 7654
Adopted August 31, 2004

National Transportation Safety Board
490 L'Enfant Plaza, S.W.
Washington, D.C. 20594

National Transportation Safety Board. 2004. U.S. Towboat *Robert Y. Love* Allision With Interstate 40 Highway Bridge Near Webbers Falls, Oklahoma, May 26, 2002. Highway/Marine Accident Report NTSB/HAR-04/05. Washington, DC.

Abstract: About 0745, on May 26, 2002, the towboat *Robert Y. Love*, pushing two empty asphalt tank barges, was traveling northbound on the McClellan-Kerr Arkansas River Navigation System, near Webbers Falls, Oklahoma. As the tow approached the Interstate 40 highway bridge at mile 360.3, it veered off course and rammed a pier 201 feet west of (outside) the navigation channel. The impact collapsed a 503-foot section of the bridge, which fell into the river and onto the barges below. According to witnesses, highway traffic continued to drive into the void in the bridge created by the collapsed spans. When traffic stopped, eight passenger vehicles and three truck tractor-semitrailer combinations had fallen into the river or onto the collapsed portions of the bridge. The accident resulted in 14 fatalities and 5 injuries and caused an estimated $30.1 million in damage to the bridge, including the operation of detours, and $276,000 in damage to the barges.

The major safety issues discussed in this report include the captain's incapacitation and countermeasures for such an event; bridge protection, including risk assessment; and mitigation of loss of life, including motorist warning systems. As a result of this accident, the National Transportation Safety Board makes recommendations to the U.S. Coast Guard, the Federal Highway Administration, and the American Association of State Highway and Transportation Officials.

Contents

Acronyms and Abbreviations

AASHTO	American Association of State Highway and Transportation Officials
ADT	average daily traffic count
ARTCO	American River Transportation Company
ASTM	American Association for Testing and Materials
AWO	American Waterways Operators
BEC	Blubaugh Engineering Company
BMS	bridge management system
CAMI	Civil Aerospace Medical Institute
CEMS	Crew Endurance Management System
CFR	*Code of Federal Regulations*
DOT	U.S. Department of Transportation
EMS	emergency medical service
EPS	electrophysiological study
FDOT	Florida Department of Transportation
FHWA	Federal Highway Administration
GPS	global positioning system
I-40	Interstate 40
I-40 bridge	Interstate 40 highway bridge
ICD	implantable cardioverter defibrillator
ISTEA	Intermodal Surface Transportation Efficiency Act of 1991
Louisiana DOTD	Louisiana Department of Transportation and Development
LMR	Lower Mississippi River
LRFD	load and resistance factor design
M-KARNS	McClellan-Kerr Arkansas River Navigation System
MMT	Magnolia Marine Transport Company
MUTCD	*Manual on Uniform Traffic Control Devices*
NBI	National Bridge Inventory
ODOT	Oklahoma Department of Transportation
PCP	phencyclidine
PI	point of intersection
RCP	Responsible Carrier Program

SHM	Structural Health Monitoring
STRAHNET	Strategic Highway Network
UMR	Upper Mississippi River
USACE	U.S. Army Corps of Engineers
U.S.C.	*United States Code*
Vessel Collision Guide Specifications	*Guide Specification and Commentary for Vessel Collision Design of Highway Bridges*
WGS 84	World Geodetic System 1984

Executive Summary

About 0745, on May 26, 2002, the towboat *Robert Y. Love*, pushing two empty asphalt tank barges, was traveling northbound on the McClellan-Kerr Arkansas River Navigation System, near Webbers Falls, Oklahoma. As the tow approached the Interstate 40 highway bridge at mile 360.3, it veered off course and rammed a pier 201 feet west of (outside) the navigation channel. The impact collapsed a 503-foot section of the bridge, which fell into the river and onto the barges below. According to witnesses, highway traffic continued to drive into the void in the bridge created by the collapsed spans. When traffic stopped, eight passenger vehicles and three truck tractor-semitrailer combinations had fallen into the river or onto the collapsed portions of the bridge. The accident resulted in 14 fatalities and 5 injuries and caused an estimated $30.1 million in damage to the bridge, including the operation of detours, and $276,000 in damage to the barges.

The National Transportation Safety Board determines that the probable cause of the *Robert Y. Love's* allision with the Interstate 40 highway bridge and its subsequent collapse was the captain's loss of consciousness, possibly as the result of an unforeseeable abnormal heart rhythm. Contributing to the loss of life was the inability of motorists to detect the collapsed bridge in time to stop their vehicles.

Major safety issues identified in this accident include:

• The captain's incapacitation and countermeasures for such an event;

• Bridge protection, including risk assessment; and

• Mitigation of loss of life, including motorist warning systems.

As a result of this accident, the National Transportation Safety Board makes recommendations to the U.S. Coast Guard, the Federal Highway Administration, and the American Association of State Highway and Transportation Officials.

Factual Information

Accident Narrative

About 0745,[1] on May 26, 2002, the towboat *Robert Y. Love*, pushing two empty asphalt tank barges, was traveling northbound on the McClellan-Kerr Arkansas River Navigation System (M-KARNS),[2] near Webbers Falls, Oklahoma. As the tow approached the Interstate 40 highway bridge at mile 360.3, it veered off course and rammed a pier 201 feet west of (outside) the navigation channel. The impact collapsed a 503-foot section of the bridge, which fell into the river and onto the barges below. According to witnesses, highway traffic continued to drive into the void in the bridge created by the collapsed spans. When traffic stopped, eight passenger vehicles and three truck tractor-semitrailer combinations had fallen into the river or onto the collapsed portions of the bridge. The accident resulted in 14 fatalities and 5 injuries and caused an estimated $30.1 million in damage to the bridge, including the operation of detours, and $276,000 in damage to the barges.

Robert Y. Love

At 0340 on May 19, 2002, the towboat *Robert Y. Love* departed Decatur, Alabama, mile 299, Tennessee River, en route to Catoosa, Oklahoma, pushing ahead two empty 297-foot-long asphalt tank barges (*MM-60* and *MM-62*), side by side (108 feet total width), with a draft[3] of 1 foot. (See figures 1 through 3.) On board were the licensed master (captain) and pilot[4] and four unlicensed crewmembers—a chief engineer, two mates, and one deckhand. On May 21, a third empty barge, *MM-54B*, was added to the tow at mile 4, Tennessee River; on May 22, *MM-54B* was removed from the tow at Rosedale Fleet, mile 585, LMR.[5] (See figure 3, locations 2 and 3.) On May 23, the tow entered M-KARNS at mile 599, LMR, heading northwest toward Catoosa on the Verdigris River, mile 444.8, M-KARNS. (See figure 3, locations 4 and 5, and figure 4.)

---

[1] All times in this report are central daylight time based on the 24-hour clock.

[2] On U.S. Army Corps of Engineers (USACE) river navigation charts, river miles along the M-KARNS are measured from mile 0, where the M-KARNS enters the Lower Mississippi River (LMR), westward for 444.8 miles to the head of navigation on the Verdigris River at Catoosa, Oklahoma. The M-KARNS flows southeastward from the Rocky Mountains in Colorado and enters the LMR at mile 599. (All miles are statute miles of 5,280 feet.) USACE controls the use and administration of the structures (bank protection, shore facility permits, regulation of water flow, and operation of the lock and dams).

[3] *Draft* refers to the depth measured from the waterline to the lowest immersed part of hull or bottom of keel.

[4] In accordance with standard marine terminology for river towboats, the terms captain and pilot are used to differentiate between the two licensed operators who navigate a vessel. The captain is the senior licensed operator of uninspected towing vessels and is in charge of the vessel. The captain stands the 0600-1200 and the 1800-2400 watches, and the pilot stands the alternate watches; the watch schedule may vary depending on company policy or boat operator's preference. Each operator is required to have a U.S. Coast Guard (Coast Guard) license as master of uninspected towing vessels for the waters on which the vessel operates.

[5] For navigation purposes, the Mississippi River is divided into the LMR and the Upper Mississippi River (UMR). The LMR extends north from the Gulf of Mexico to the confluence of the Ohio River. The UMR extends north from the Ohio River to the head of navigation at Minneapolis, Minnesota.

Figure 1. Towboat *Robert Y. Love.* (Source: Magnolia Marine Transport Company)

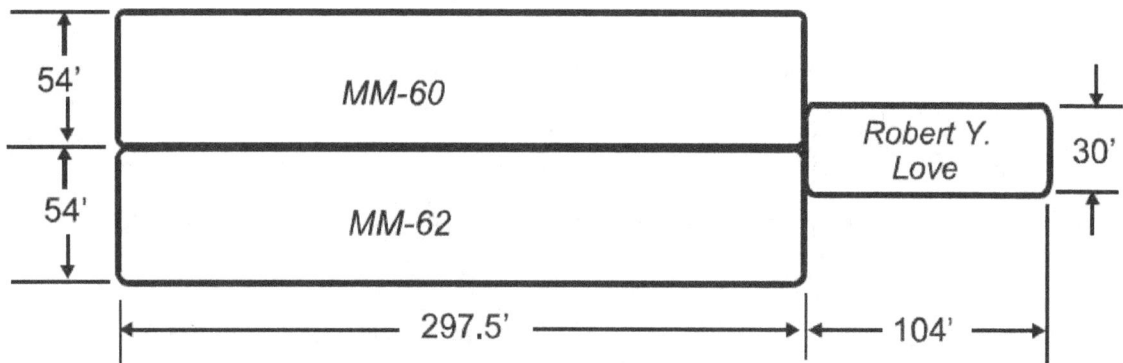

Figure 2. Schematic of towboat *Robert Y. Love* and barge tow.

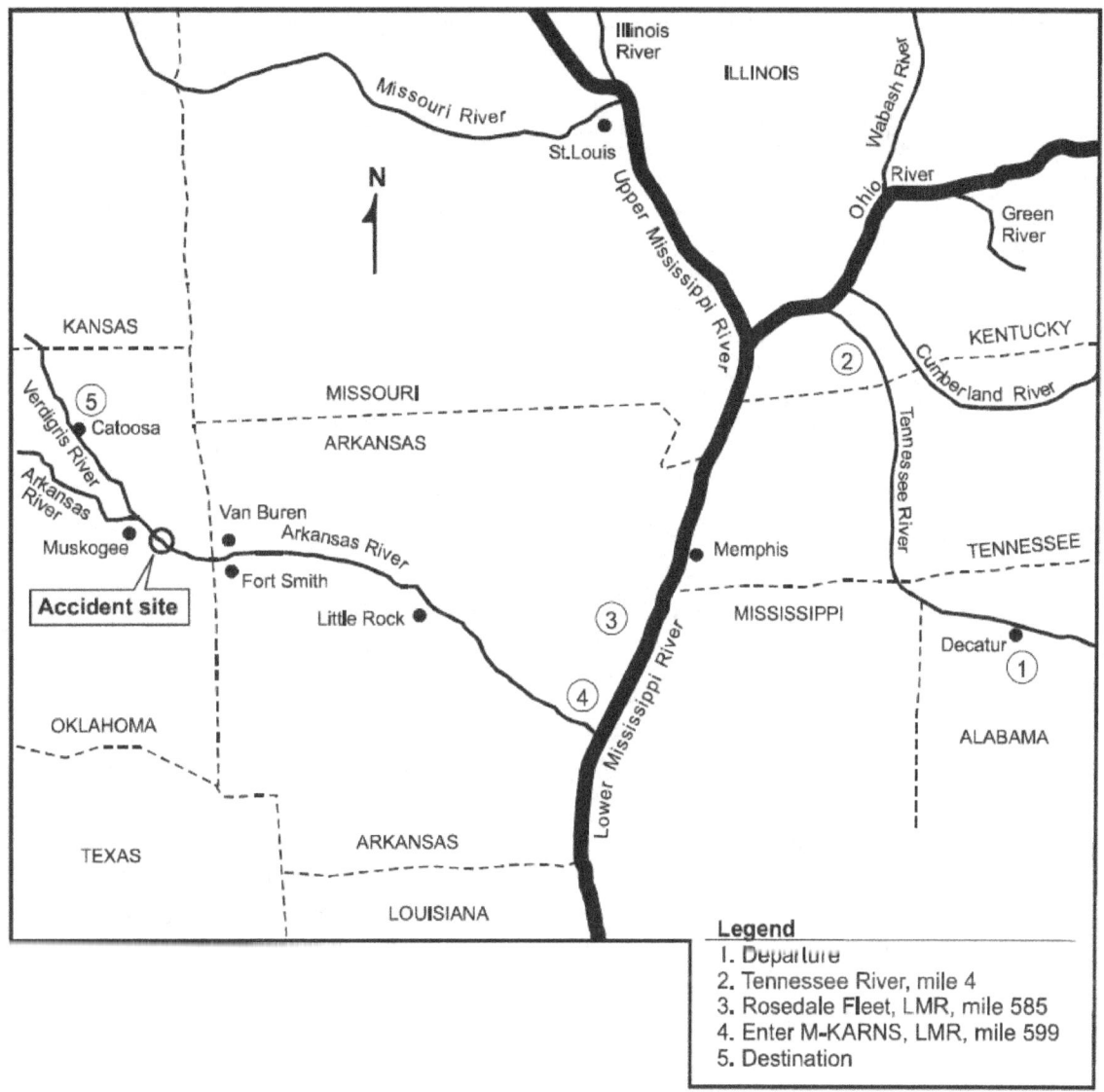

Figure 3. Map showing origin, selected locations, and destination of tow.

On May 25, about 1840, while the tow was at lock 13 (near Van Buren, Arkansas), mile 292.8, M-KARNS, the alternate captain departed on vacation and was relieved by the regular captain. The regular captain took the navigation watch about 1910 and was relieved at the end of the watch by the pilot about 2245 on May 25. On May 26, about 0530, the pilot was, in turn, relieved by the captain.

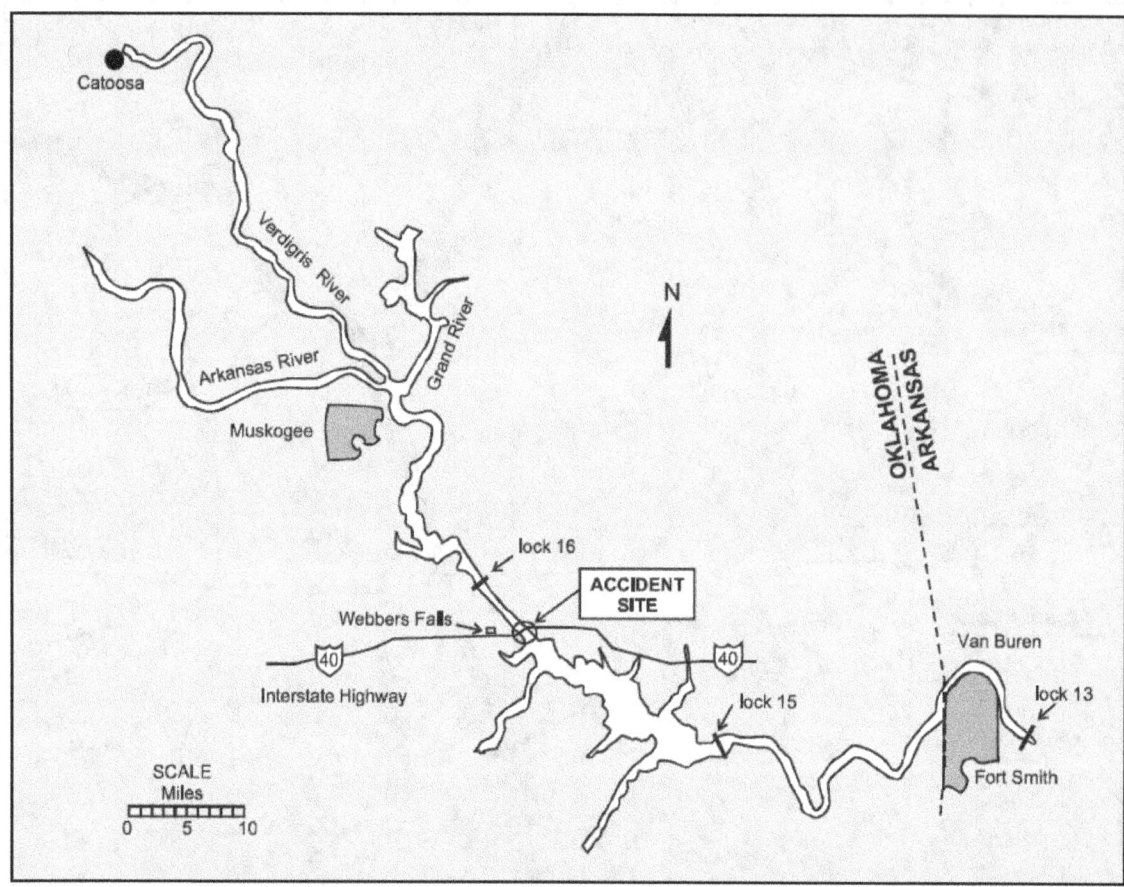

Figure 4. McClellan-Kerr Arkansas River Navigation System from Fort Smith, Arkansas, to head of navigation at Catoosa, Oklahoma.

About 0700 on May 26, the on-duty deckhand went to the wheelhouse to clean the deck. Afterward, he had a conversation with the captain for about 25 to 30 minutes and left the wheelhouse. The deckhand later stated that the captain "didn't seem like he was sick or anything wrong with him or anything." The captain instructed the deckhand to awaken the relief mate (mate) because the vessel was approaching lock 16, mile 366.6, which was about 1 hour away.[6] (See figure 4.)

The mate stated the deckhand awakened him about 0725. The deckhand then placed some trash in the bin on the stern[7] of the towboat and emptied the mop water in the engineroom sink. When the deckhand returned to the galley, the mate was there, and they were talking and drinking coffee when they felt an impact and the refrigerators and other galley equipment fell to the deck. They said they then heard a "big bang," went outside the galley, and saw a tractor-semitrailer and a pickup truck drive off the Interstate 40 (I-40)

---

[6] According to 33 *Code of Federal Regulations* (CFR) 207.275, two deckhands—in this instance, a relief mate and a deckhand—are required to be on the tow to handle lines while the tow maneuvers through the lock.

[7] In marine usage, the *stern* of the boat is the rear, and the *bow* is the front.

highway bridge (I-40 bridge) and land in the water. They also saw a collapsed section of the bridge deck hanging at an angle from the bridge and resting on the bow end of the barges in the tow. (See figures 5 through 7.)

Figure 5. View of accident scene from downstream (southern) approach to bridge.

Figure 6. View of accident scene from edge of remaining eastbound span.

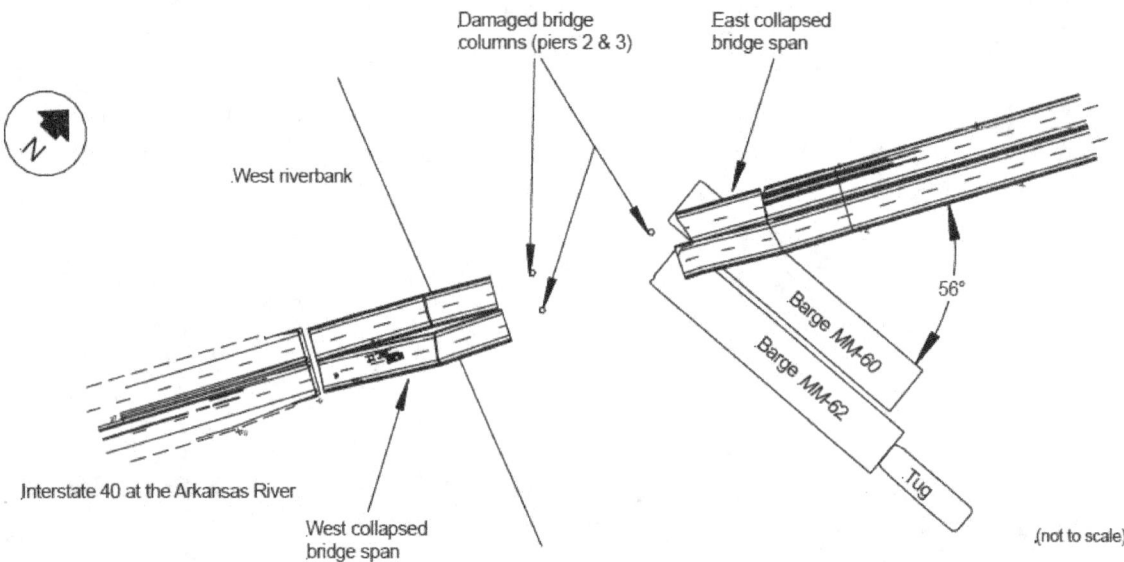

Figure 7. Accident damage.

The captain stated that after he told the deckhand to awaken the mate, he watched to make sure the deckhand walked safely down the stairs from the wheelhouse, then returned his attention to maneuvering the tow. The captain reported that the last thing he remembered before the accident was aligning the tow to pass under the I-40 bridge main navigation span (between piers 4 and 5) and passing a green navigation buoy (channel marker) to port[8] approximately 0.35 miles from the bridge.[9]

After the accident, the captain stated that his unconsciousness occurred "all at once" and further stated, "I remember looking out to the side of the buoy and then looking back at the bridge, and after that I don't remember nothing." His first recollection after the allision[10] was being in a crouched position between the operator's chair and the vessel control console and realizing that his head and arm were wet from the soft drink he had placed on the console. (See figure 8.) He stated he could not visually focus on anything at first nor "get oriented right." He managed to get to a fully standing position to be able to see over the console and out of the wheelhouse window. After he saw the highway bridge deck collapsed onto the deck of the barges, he sounded five blasts on the vessel's whistle (a mariner's danger signal). While still experiencing problems focusing upon what was happening, he recalled seeing an 18-wheeler, and possibly a pickup truck, go off the bridge. He said that he then "started blowing the [towboat's] whistle again, just to try to get somebody's attention to stop…[the traffic] on the bridge." He further explained that though he was familiar with the boat, he had to

---

[8] In marine usage, *port* is left and *starboard* is right.

[9] The Coast Guard had placed the green unlighted buoy on the left (upbound) side of the channel, about 0.05 mile (about 260 feet) to the left of the sailing line on the USACE chart, near mile 359.5, or approximately 0.35 miles (about 1,850 feet) downstream, from the bridge.

[10] In marine usage, *allision* refers to a moving ship striking a stationary ship or other stationary object.

"fumble around for the general alarm[11] to get it set off." The captain could not recall the allision. He said that he had applied a few degrees of left rudder to align the tow for passage through the bridge navigation span and that when he regained consciousness, the rudder was still in the left position.

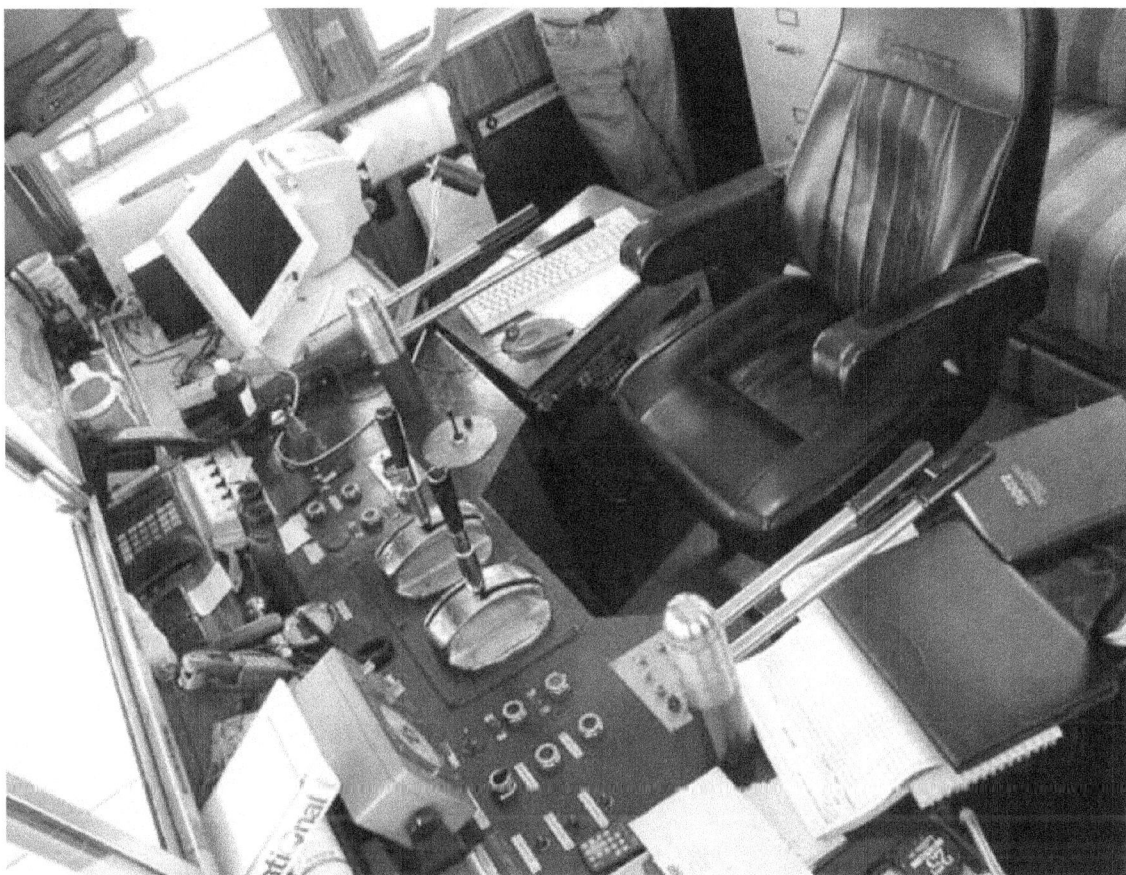

Figure 8. *Robert Y. Love* wheelhouse, showing captain's chair and console.

The mate who was on duty indicated that he ran from the galley to the wheelhouse and when he got to the door, the captain was saying, "make them stop, why won't they stop coming [referring to the vehicles on the bridge]." The captain asked the mate, the first person to arrive in the wheelhouse, to send a distress message to the Coast Guard. The mate made the call on the VHF-FM radio (channel 16) and then telephoned the company office on the company cellular telephone to report the allision. The radio distress call was heard and logged at 0745, simultaneously, by the watchstander at Coast Guard Group Lower Mississippi River (Group LMR), Memphis, Tennessee, and by the lock operator at lock 15, mile 336.2. (See figure 4.)

---

[11] The general alarm is an internal emergency alarm system, activated from the wheelhouse, that sounds throughout the towboat to warn the crew of an urgent situation on board the vessel.

The remainder of the crew heard the towboat's whistle sound, followed by the sounding of the general alarm bell. While making routine engine room rounds, the chief engineer heard the bell. He reported hearing the accident about 0750 and that the impact caused him to fall to one knee. He immediately returned to the engineroom to check void spaces for flooding and was in the engineroom for 10 to 15 minutes. The engineer stated that he did not notice any engine speed changes before the accident and that had the engine speeds changed before the accident, he would have easily noticed the change.

The pilot and the other mate were off duty and asleep in their quarters during the allision. The pilot, who was in his bed when he felt a bump, heard the towboat's whistle sounding and then heard the general alarm sound. He looked out of his window (his room was on the port side of the main deck, aft) and saw the bridge deck lying on the barges. He said he immediately ran out of the deckhouse and went to the head of the tow to check the condition of the barges. About 45 seconds to a minute and a half later, after checking the tow, the pilot arrived in the wheelhouse and found: "The captain was visibly shaken...He was standing, and he was in tears, shaken." The pilot then relieved the captain from watch and the mate from handling communications. The mate and the pilot stated that the captain told them that he had passed out, that he did not hear or see the impact, and that the last thing that he remembered was seeing the deckhand walk out of the wheelhouse.

The pilot stated he heard people in the water yelling for help, so he directed the mate and chief engineer to put the vessel's motorboat into the water to determine whether they could render assistance. The mate and chief engineer searched for survivors for about 30 minutes, saw a recreational boat rescue one person, and then returned to the towboat without rescuing anyone.

Highway Vehicles on Bridge

Eleven vehicles carrying 19 occupants either collapsed with or drove off the bridge. A tractor-semitrailer driver stated that he had been heading westbound on the bridge at 70 mph and had his windows up. He was traveling in the right lane, and no other vehicles were around him. He stated that as he came up over the rise in the bridge, the roadway was gone and the next thing he recalled seeing was a large exposed bridge support pillar. He then recalled being in the water and trying to grab debris to stay afloat. Some nearby boaters threw him a cushion and then picked him up in their boat. He said he could hear another man yelling for help and saw another boat pick up that man. An eastbound pickup truck drove off the bridge and hit the collapsed bridge span but stopped before driving into the water. (See figure 9.) The pickup's two occupants were rescued from the bridge. Nine other vehicles either went down with the spans that collapsed or drove off the bridge.

Figure 9. Eastbound pickup that drove off bridge onto collapsed span but stopped before driving into void.

Recreational Boats

At the time of the accident, a fishing tournament was underway out of Webbers Falls (2.6 river miles upstream of the I-40 bridge). One of the contestants observed the *Robert Y. Love* and tow headed to the west bank of the river, outside the main navigation span. He indicated that after the tow struck the bridge supports, the span collapsed immediately. Another pair of contestants, who were upriver of the bridge when they heard a loud boom, observed a section of the bridge span collapse and a number of vehicles enter the water. The operator of this boat said that he saw at least one vehicle fall with the bridge and he then accelerated his boat toward the bridge, and reached the area in about 20 seconds. He also stated that he saw two more vehicles drive off the bridge and called 911, reaching the Muskogee Police Department. After the call, he saw five more vehicles drive off the bridge. He indicated that most, if not all, of these vehicles came from the westbound lanes. When the boat was about 30 to 40 yards upstream, he fired a flare from a hand-held flare pistol toward the bridge, in front of a tractor-trailer truck traveling from the east side of the bridge to the west side, to warn the driver of the danger. The truckdriver stopped, before reaching the edge of the collapsed span, partially jackknifing on the roadway. Vehicles behind this truck stopped before reaching the tractor-trailer truck. The same recreational boat then rescued a person in the water near the bow of one barge. The boat occupants saw two other recreational boats, also from the tournament; each of them rescued a person from the water. In all, three survivors were rescued from the water. The recreational boats took the three survivors to a boat ramp at Webbers Falls, where they waited for emergency medical service (EMS) personnel to arrive on scene.

Emergency Response

At 0748, the Muskogee Police Department received the first of approximately 25 calls regarding a bridge collapse at I-40 and the Arkansas River with several vehicles in the water. Seven local police departments[12] responded, as well as the Oklahoma Highway Patrol and the Muskogee Police Department. Six ambulances responded; the first arrived on scene at 0756. In addition, 17 local fire departments,[13] 10 EMS departments,[14] 8 emergency management agencies,[15] 7 State agencies,[16] and 7 Federal agencies,[17] for a total of 58 local, State, and Federal agencies, responded to this accident.

After receiving the distress call from the *Robert Y. Love*, the watchstander at Coast Guard Group LMR sent an urgent marine information broadcast at 0746 over VHF-FM radio channel 16 advising mariners of the accident. He then used the Group's bridge allision checklist and contacted the Arkansas State Police, who advised that they had called the Muskogee Police Department and had other units en route to the bridge at 0747. The Coast Guard watchstander then notified the 8th Coast Guard District office, New Orleans, Louisiana, which is the next senior operational command over the Coast Guard Group LMR. He also notified the Coast Guard Marine Safety Office, Memphis,

---

[12] Muskogee County Sheriff's Department sheriff and deputies, Gans Police Department, Gore Police Department, Checotah Police Department, McIntosh County Sheriff's Office, Tulsa Police Department, and Fort Gibson Police Department.

[13] Muskogee Fire Department, Ash Creek Fire Department, Fort Gibson Fire Department, Wilburton Fire Department, Porum Fire Department, Warner Volunteer Fire Department, Norwood Fire Department, Sallisaw Fire Department, Spring Valley Fire Department, Keota Fire Department, Texanna Fire Department, West End Fire Department, Checotah Fire and Emergency Management, Tulsa Fire Department, Vian Fire Department, Onapa Fire Department, and the Oklahoma City Fire Department.

[14] Muskogee County, Fort Gibson, Warner, Haskell, Cherokee County, Sequoyah County, Northeast Oklahoma Underwater Recovery, Washington County Rescue, Vian First Responder, and McIntosh Office of Emergency Services.

[15] Muskogee City Emergency Operations Center, Muskogee County Emergency Management, Grove Emergency Management, Washington County Emergency Operations Center, Cherokee County Emergency Management, Haskell County Emergency Management, Pittsburg County Emergency Management, and Sequoyah County Emergency Management.

[16] Oklahoma Department of Public Safety Communications, Oklahoma Department of Transportation, Oklahoma Office of Emergency Management, Oklahoma National Guard, State Medical Examiners Office, Department of Environmental Quality, and Oklahoma State Bureau of Investigations.

[17] USACE, the Federal Highway Administration, the U.S. Environmental Protection Agency, the U.S. Fish and Wildlife Service, the Coast Guard Gulf Strike Team, the U.S. National Guard, and the National Weather Service.

Tennessee, which is responsible for marine safety activities on the Arkansas River. At 0846, the Captain of the Port, Memphis,[18] ordered the river closed to vessel traffic from mile 357 to 363, Arkansas River. At 1100, the Captain of the Port, Memphis, issued a safety marine information broadcast advising mariners that diving operations for vehicles and occupants were being conducted at the I-40 bridge, mile 360.3, Arkansas River. The broadcast further directed search and rescue units to "transit the area at the slowest safe speed possible and transit with extreme caution."

Injuries

The following table is based on the International Civil Aviation Organization's injury criteria, which the National Transportation Safety Board uses in accident reports for all transportation modes.

Table 1. Injuries.

Injury type	Drivers	Passengers	Vessel crew	Total
Fatal	7	7	0	14
Serious	2	1	0	3
Minor	2	0	0	2
None	0	0	6	6
Total	11	8	6	25

Title 49 CFR 830.2 defines *fatal injury* as "any injury which results in death within 30 days of the accident" and *serious injury* as "an injury which: (1) requires hospitalization for more than 48 hours, commencing within 7 days from the date the injury was received; (2) results in a fracture of any bone (except simple fractures of fingers, toes, or nose); (3) causes severe hemorrhages, nerve, or tendon damage; (4) involves any internal organ; or (5) involves second- or third-degree burns, or any burn affecting more than 5 percent of the body surface."

Damage

The *Robert Y. Love* did not sustain any damage. Its barges sustained a total of $275,554 in repair costs (barge *MM-60*, $113,478; barge *MM-62*, $162,076). The barge repairs were completed on July 15 and 22, 2002, respectively.

The impact collapsed a 503-foot section of the bridge and two piers. During the repair to the bridge, the Oklahoma Department of Transportation (ODOT) operated a separate detour for the I-40 traffic in both directions. The westbound detour was 8 miles and added an additional 4 miles to the trip. In addition, traffic had to negotiate four right-angle turns and traverse two railroad crossings[19] while passing through two small cities. The eastbound detour was about 78 miles and added an additional 30 miles to the trip.

---

[18] The commanding officer at the Marine Safety Office, Memphis, is also designated by the Commandant, U.S. Coast Guard, as Officer in Charge of Marine Inspection (for regulating the commercial marine industry by conducting inspections and investigations) and Captain of the Port (for conducting pollution control and port safety duties).

According to ODOT, numerous bridges along the detour route had to be repaired and monitored to accommodate the interstate commercial traffic volumes. The bridge reopened for traffic on July 29, 2002, 65 days after the accident. ODOT estimated that the total cost of the bridge repairs, including operating the detours, was $30.1 million.

Crew Information

The *Robert Y. Love* had a crew of six, including the captain and the pilot, who both held licenses in accordance with U.S. law. The remainder of the crew was not required to hold a Coast Guard license.

Captain

The captain, age 60 at the time of the accident, began his marine career on the Mississippi River in November 1957 and for about 40 years had been working in various capacities on board inland towing vessels operating on the Western Rivers[20] of the United States. He started as a deckhand, serving in that capacity through the 1960s before being assigned to the wheelhouse for training as a vessel operator. On May 21, 1973, he obtained his original Coast Guard license as operator of uninspected towing vessels.[21] In 1991, he went to work for Magnolia Marine Transport Company (MMT), the owner of the *Robert Y. Love*, serving as a pilot, relief captain, and captain of its vessels. He had been the captain of the *Robert Y. Love* since February 22, 2001. At the time of this accident, he held a Coast Guard license as an operator of uninspected towing vessels upon the Great Lakes and Inland Waters with a radar observer (unlimited) endorsement. His current license had been issued in December 1997 and was due to expire in December 2002. In December 1997, he completed a radar observer (unlimited) training course to renew the radar endorsement on his license, as required by Coast Guard regulations.

---

[19] About 18 to 20 trains per day traversed these rail crossings; the trains were more than 100 cars long and loaded with coal destined for an electrical generating facility.

[20] The Western Rivers consist of the Mississippi River and all of its tributaries and connecting waterways, the Gulf Intracoastal Waterways, and the other navigable river systems that empty into the Gulf of Mexico.

[21] The Towing Vessel Licensing Act of July 7, 1972, requires that all commercial vessels 26 or more feet long engaged, or intended to be engaged, in the service of towing be under the direction and control of persons licensed by the Coast Guard.

Captain's 72-Hour History

The captain's activities and hours of rest before the accident, based upon information collected during Safety Board interviews with both the captain and the crew, are summarized in figure 10 and in tables 2 and 3.

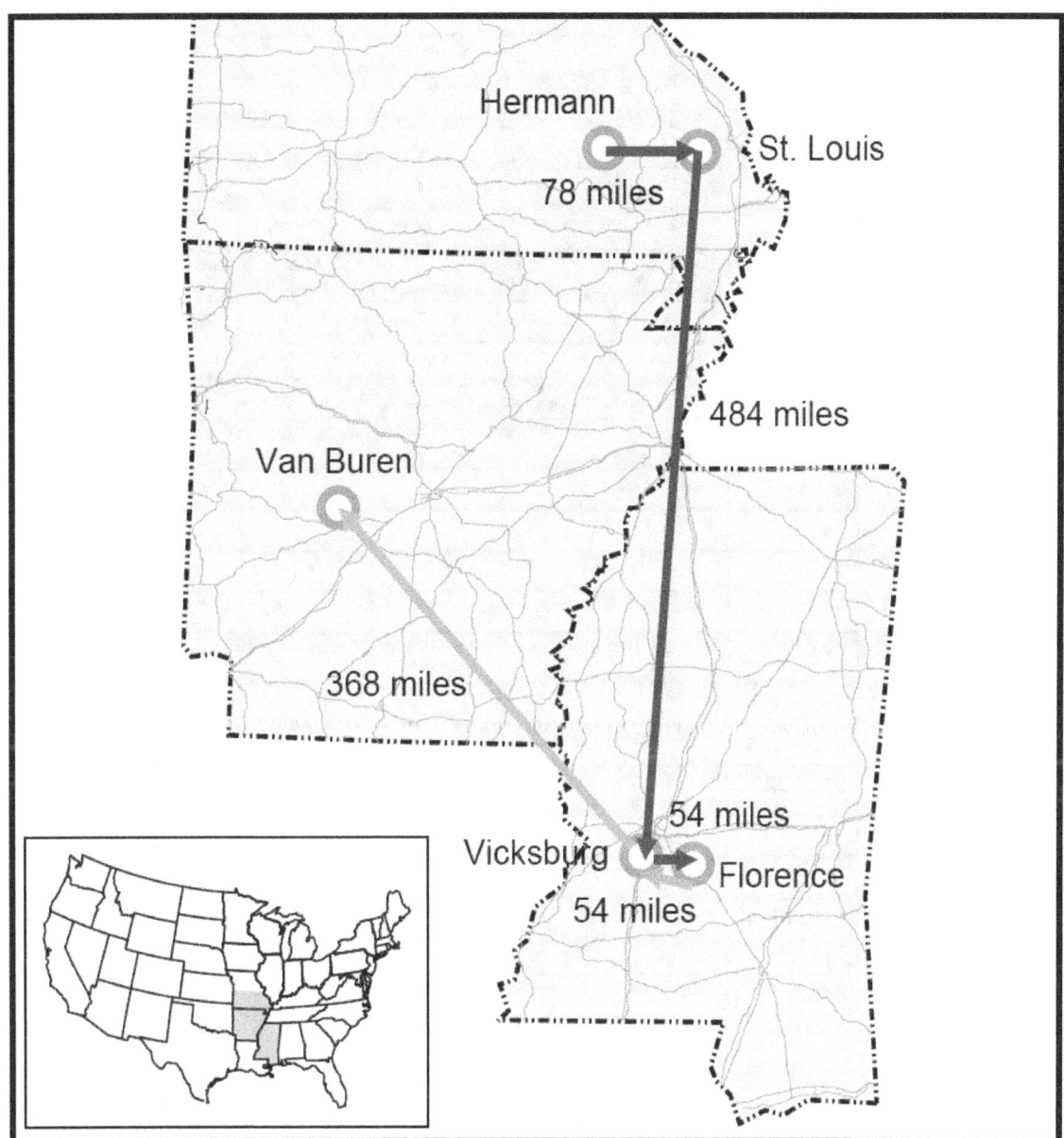

Figure 10. Captain's automobile travel preceding accident.

Table 2. Captain's 72-hour history.

Date	Time	Event
May 23, 2002	0500	Onboard *Jennie Dehmer* on the Missouri River. Woke up and had ice water.
	0600-1100	Went to the wheelhouse and remained there, speaking with the relief pilot.
	1100	Ate lunch.
	1200	Went to bed.
	1600	Woke up, showered, and ate. After eating, went to the wheelhouse to speak to the relief pilot.
	2300	Went to galley for a snack and a glass of tea and then went to bed.
May 24, 2002	0500	Woke up, went to galley for a glass of water, and then to wheelhouse.
	1045	Ate lunch, went to wheelhouse, and then went to bed.
	1430	Woke up to prepare to leave the *Jennie Dehmer*.
	1600	Departed the *Jennie Dehmer* at Hermann, Missouri, and drove 78 miles to the St. Louis airport with two crewmembers.
	1900	Dropped off one crewmember; the other took over driving.
May 25, 2002	0300	Arrived in Vicksburg, Mississippi, switched from the company car to a personal car, and continued to the captain's home (484 miles from St. Louis airport to Vicksburg, Mississippi).
	0415	Arrived at captain's home in Florence, Mississippi (54 miles from Vicksburg to Florence).
	0500	Went to bed.
	0830	Woke up and ate some fruit.
	1010	Left Florence and drove 54 miles to Vicksburg.
	1115	Departed Vicksburg en route to lock 13 (near Van Buren, Arkansas).
	1840	Met the *Robert Y. Love* at lock 13 (approximately 368 miles from Vicksburg).
	1910-1915	Assumed watch aboard the *Robert Y. Love*.
	2230-2245	Relieved by the pilot.
	2315-2330	Went to the galley for a snack, took two Benadryl® capsules for a sinus headache, and then went to bed.
May 26, 2002	0500	Woke up and went to galley for a soft drink.
	0515-0520	Began watch.
	0700-0730	Had a 25- to 30-minute conversation in the wheelhouse with the deckhand, who had been cleaning. Captain instructed the deckhand to leave the wheelhouse to wake up mate.
	0745	Allision of the *Robert Y. Love* and tow with the I-40 bridge.

Table 3. Captain's hours of rest in 72 hours before accident.

Rest period	Date	Times	Hours of rest
1	May 23	1200 to 1600	4.0
2	May 23-24	2300-2330 to 0500	5.5-6.0
3	May 24	1100-1130 to 1430	3.0-3.5
4	May 25	0500 to 0830	3.5
5	May 25-26	2315-2330 to 0500	5.5-5.75
Total			21.50 –22.75

The captain stated that his duty (work) rotation was 30 days on and 15 days off and that he had stood the normal captain's watches of 0600-1200 and 1800-2400 since coming to the towboat *Robert Y. Love* in 2001. He further stated that "after 44 years," he was accustomed to the "6-on/6-off" duty schedule used on river towboats.

Operations

MMT owns and operates 16 towboats and about 60 barges and has been in the inland towing business for 32 years, according to the company's Director of Operations. It employs about 220 people, of whom 185 are vessel employees; the other 35 serve in shoreside management and other positions. The company's primary business is transporting products such as asphalt or black oil through the Mississippi River system and intracoastal waterways of the Gulf of Mexico.

According to company officials, MMT vessels performed 711 round trips on inland waterways during the fiscal year ending June 30, 2004.

Vessel Information

The *Robert Y. Love* was a conventional twin-screw, diesel-driven, uninspected,[22] inland river towboat. The vessel was constructed of steel, 104 feet long, and had a beam (width) of 30 feet. It had an operating draft of 7 feet 9 inches and had a displacement[23] of 444.5 long tons (a long ton equals 2,240 pounds). The vessel was built in 1955 by the Nashville Bridge Company and the Alabama Dry Dock & Shipbuilding Company, Mobile, Alabama. Its first owner, the Canal Barge Company, named the vessel *Caroline*. In 1991, the vessel was sold to its present owner, MMT, Jackson, Mississippi, and renamed. In 1992, the vessel's main engines were replaced, increasing the horsepower from 1800 to 2400 rpm.

The *Robert Y. Love* had a retractable or variable-height wheelhouse that could be raised or lowered using a hydraulic ram system. In waterways where wheelhouse height was not restricted by bridge vertical clearance or other structures, the wheelhouse could be raised to the highest position for greater visibility. When necessary for the vessel to pass under a bridge with limited vertical clearance or to avoid waiting for a bridge to open, the wheelhouse could be lowered to a point where the lowest eye height was about 16 feet and the top of the wheelhouse was 17.5 feet above the waterline. Maximum eye height with the wheelhouse in the raised position was 29.5 feet; the overall maximum height with antennas extended vertically was 43 feet. At the time of the accident, the wheelhouse was in the raised position.

---

[22] An uninspected vessel is not subject to Coast Guard inspection under 46 *United States Code* (U.S.C.). The following categories of vessels are subject to inspection: freight vessels, nautical school vessels, ships, offshore supply vessels, passenger vessels, sailing school vessels, seagoing barges, seagoing motor vessels, small passenger vessels, steam vessels, tank vessels, fish processing vessels, fish tender vessels, Great Lakes barges, and oil spill response vessels.

[23] Volume or weight of the fluid displaced by a vessel.

The wheelhouse was equipped with two VHF-FM radiotelephones, a single side-band radio, radar, a global positioning system unit, swing meter, depth sounder, steering controls, and engine controls. The vessel also had a steering rudder aft and flanking rudders[24] forward of each of the two propellers.

The Director of Marine Engineering for MMT reported that the *Robert Y. Love* had been through its annual drydocking in March 2002. The company and crew conducted hull, steering machinery, engine, and electrical equipment inspections. They reported that the results were satisfactory.

The double-hull tank barges *MM-60* and *MM-62* built in Ashland City, Tennessee, in 1999, were owned by the MMT and had identical dimensions: 297.5 feet long, beam of 54.0 feet, and an empty draft of 1 foot. According to the barge's "Strength and Stability Calculations,"[25] at a draft of 1 foot, *MM-60* had a displacement of 402.6 long tons and *MM-62* had a displacement of 427.4 long tons. Each barge had eight cargo tanks, four to port and four to starboard, separated by a centerline bulkhead. Each barge had a 6-million-BTU thermal fluid heater on deck, aft. The barge sterns were box-shaped and the bows were raked to present a streamlined underwater shape to reduce water resistance. Each had a gross tonnage of 1,619 and a maximum loaded draft of 11.5 feet. Both vessels had last been inspected and issued a 5-year certificate of inspection by the Coast Guard Marine Safety Office, St. Louis, Missouri, on August 23, 2001. The vessels were certified to carry up to 25,800 barrels[26] of Grade A through Grade E cargoes.[27] The cargo thermal fluid heaters were allowed to be operated only when the vessels were carrying Grade E cargoes, such as asphalt.

Postaccident inspection of the tow revealed a large indentation on the port side of the bow of barge *MM-60*. The indentation in the headlog, 10 feet from the corner, was 2 feet wide and 1 foot deep. (See figures 11A and 11B.)

Waterway Information

The Arkansas River is part of the M-KARNS, which is operated by USACE. The M-KARNS begins in Arkansas at the confluence of the White River, mile 599, LMR. It continues west on the man-made Arkansas Post Canal and then up the Arkansas River, into Oklahoma (see figure 4) to mile 395, at the junction of the Verdigris River at Muskogee, and then onward to the Verdigris River to the head of navigation at Catoosa, mile 444.8.

---

[24] Also known as *backing rudders*, these are usually smaller rudders installed forward of the propeller and used for maneuvering when the propellers are turning astern, regardless of the actual movement of the towboat.

[25] Trinity Marine Product, Ashland City Yard, Trinity Tag 96025, Hulls 4342 and 4343, March 2, 1999.

[26] A barrel equals 42 U.S. gallons.

[27] Flammable or combustible substances as defined by American Society for Testing and Materials (ASTM) Standard D323. Grade E cargo is any combustible liquid having a flashpoint of 150° F or above. The ASTM standard defines asphalt as an example of a Grade E combustible liquid.

Figure 11A. Port side of headlog of barge *MM-60* showing the indentation made by south column of pier 3.

Figure 11B. Overhead view of indentation.

Construction of the M-KARNS began in May 1952; the system became operational in 1970. Each year, approximately 12 million tons of commodities are transported on the waterway.[28] Total domestic tonnage on all U.S. internal waterways is about 620 million tons per year.[29]

The waterway has 17 locks and dams, 12 in Arkansas and 5 in Oklahoma, that step the water levels up a total of 420 feet in elevation. Thirty-eight bridges cross the waterway. USACE maintains a minimum 9-foot channel depth on the system, and the Coast Guard marks the river with buoys and daymarks.[30]

From mile 357 of the M-KARNS, about 3 miles downriver from the I-40 bridge, the channel makes a gradual right turn of approximately 70 degrees over a distance of about 1 mile. The channel then straightens out for about a mile and then makes a slight left turn of about 10 to 15 degrees, about 0.40 miles from the bridge.

The Robert S. Kerr Lock and Dam (lock 15), mile 336.2, is 24.1 miles below (downstream of) the I-40 bridge. The Webbers Falls Lock and Dam (lock 16), mile 366.6, is 6.3 miles upstream of the I-40 bridge. (See figure 4.) According to USACE officials, average barge traffic at each of the two locks in the vicinity of the accident site is about three tows per day.

River currents in the M-KARNS are negligible most of the year because the water levels in the system are controlled by a series of dams, which regulate the release of water into the system. The area between two successive dams is known as a pool. The USACE District Office at Tulsa, Oklahoma, determined that at the time of the accident the pool elevation was 459.37 feet (normal pool is 458 feet), and the current speed at the bridge was about 2 mph.

According to USACE M-KARNS navigation charts, the I-40 bridge has a 300-foot-wide main navigation span and a vertical clearance above normal pool of 62.4 feet. The captain of the *Robert Y. Love* stated that he had been through the I-40 bridge hundreds of times and that it was an easy bridge to navigate. He explained that once lined up, a little right rudder would be required to steady the tow before placing the rudder amidships (zero rudder angle) and passing under the navigation span.

---

[28] According to USACE, major commodities include iron and steel, chemical fertilizer and other chemicals, petroleum products, sand/gravel and rock, coke and coal, soybeans, and wheat and other grains <http://www.swl.usace.army.mil/navigation/commod.html>.

[29] USACE Waterborne Commerce Statistics Center <http://www.iwr.usace.army.mil/ndc/wcsc/wcsc00/fordom.pdf>.

[30] According the Coast Guard's U.S. Aids to Navigation System, a daymark is an identifying sign on a beacon (fixed navigational aid) that makes the beacon more readily visible in daylight <http://www.uscgboating.org/safety/aton/system.htm>.

Highway Information

I-40 and the I-40 bridge are owned and operated by ODOT. I-40 is an east-west, rural, principal arterial, controlled access, interstate highway. At the accident site, I-40 is a two-way, four-lane, divided highway. The design speed and posted speed limit were 70 mph, and the minimum-posted speed limit was 40 mph. The 2001 average daily traffic count (ADT) for both directions was 19,200 vehicles. Commercial vehicles accounted for 27 to 33 percent of the ADT during 1997 and 1999.

The concrete bridge deck had a 36-inch-high concrete barrier separating the east and westbound lanes. The traffic lanes were 12 feet wide, with 3-foot-wide inside and outside shoulders. At the immediate approach to the bridge, the highway was asphalt, with a 33-inch-high concrete barrier separating the eastbound and westbound traffic lanes. The approach lanes were also 12 feet wide, with 4.5-foot-wide inside shoulders and 15-foot-wide outside shoulders. The traffic lanes were divided by painted stripes approximately 11 feet long and spaced every 20 feet. A 4-inch-wide retroreflective painted solid yellow edgeline delineated the inside shoulder, and a 4-inch-wide retroreflective painted solid white edgeline delineated the outside shoulder. The painted lines met the line width and space requirements specified in the *Manual on Uniform Traffic Control Devices* (MUTCD).[31]

The eastbound lanes were level approaching the 1,989-foot-long bridge and transitioned into a 900-foot sag vertical curve[32] with a 3-percent grade to the point of intersection (PI) of a 1,444-foot vertical curve. (The PI of the curve was 632 feet from the west end of the bridge and 1,356 feet from the east end of the bridge.) At the PI of the vertical curve, the grade became a 2.2-percent downgrade that transitioned into a 900-foot sag vertical curve at the end of the bridge.

Bridge Information

The I-40 bridge was built in 1967 and spanned the Arkansas River at M-KARNS mile marker 360.3. Bridge plans indicate that the I-40 bridge project[33] began 2 miles west of the Arkansas River and extended east in Muskogee and Sequoyah Counties, Oklahoma, over the Arkansas River.

The Secretary of the Army approved the State of Oklahoma's bridge permit on October 22, 1963, for the location and plans of a bridge to be constructed across the Arkansas River near Webbers Falls. According to the permit, the structure was to be 1,989 feet long, with the main span providing a vertical clearance of 52 feet above flood stage and a horizontal clearance of 322 feet between the main piers. The remainder of the spans provided a vertical clearance of approximately 50 feet and a horizontal clearance between the piers of approximately 125 feet.

---

[31] The Federal Highway Administration (FHWA) approved the MUTCD as the standard for all streets and highways in accordance with 23 U.S.C., Sections 109 (b), 109 (d), 402 (a), and 23 CFR 1204.4.

[32] A vertical curve provides a smooth transition from one roadway grade to another; this transition may be a *sag* vertical curve (dip) or *crest* vertical curve (hill).

[33] Federal-aid project number I-40-6 (99) 288.

The I-40 bridge was a twin-girder, continuous-span bridge consisting of 13 concrete deck sections that were 7.5 inches thick and supported by steel girders and a steel superstructure that was, in turn, supported by 12 reinforced concrete piers and 2 bridge abutments. Piers 1 through 4 were west of the main channel, and piers 5 through 12 were east of the main channel. Piers 4 and 5 constituted the concrete piers for the main spans and navigable channel. Table 4 lists the dimensions (in feet) of the piers, including the footings, columns, and pier caps; figure 12 illustrates these pier components.

Table 4. Bridge pier components (in feet).

Pier number	Footing	Column (section 1)	Column (section 2)	Column (section 3)	Pier cap
1	12 x 17 x 6	7 x 20	6 x 30	5 x 32	5 x 66 x 7.5
2	12 x 17 x 6	7 x 21	6 x 30	5 x 34.5	5 x 66 x 7.5
3	12 x 18 x 6	7 x 21.83	6 x 30	5 x 37.16	5 x 66 x 7.5
4	24 x 55 x 7	10 x 49 x 27.33	8 x 47 x 24	6 x 45 x 23.25	6 x 66 x 12
5	24 x 55 x 7	10 x 49 x 27.33	8 x 47 x 24	6 x 45 x 24.16	6 x 66 x 12
6	12 x 18 x 6	7 x 19.83	6 x 30	5 x 37.16	5 x 66 x 7.5
7	12 x 17 x 6	7 x 19	6 x 30	5 x 34.5	5 x 66 x 7.5
8	12 x 17 x 6	7 x 19	6 x 30	5 x 32	5 x 66 x 7.5
9	12 x 17 x 6	7 x 18.25	6 x 30	5 x 29.25	5 x 66 x 7.5
10	12 x 17 x 6	7 x 16.83	6 x 30	5 x 27.16	5 x 66 x 7.5
11	12 x 17 x 6	6 x 20.83	6 x 23	5 x 23.66	5 x 66 x 7.5
12	12 x 17 x 6	6 x 21.08	6 x 23	5 x 20.91	5 x 66 x 7.5

Notes:
1. Measurements are provided as diameter and length or width, length, and height, as applicable.
2. At piers 1 through 3 and 6 through 12, each column was interconnected to adjacent columns by use of a web wall (34 feet x 2 feet x 22 feet). With the exception of the interconnection at the main channel piers 4 and 5, the web wall does not have any structural integrity and is used solely to keep drifting debris from accumulating between the pier columns.

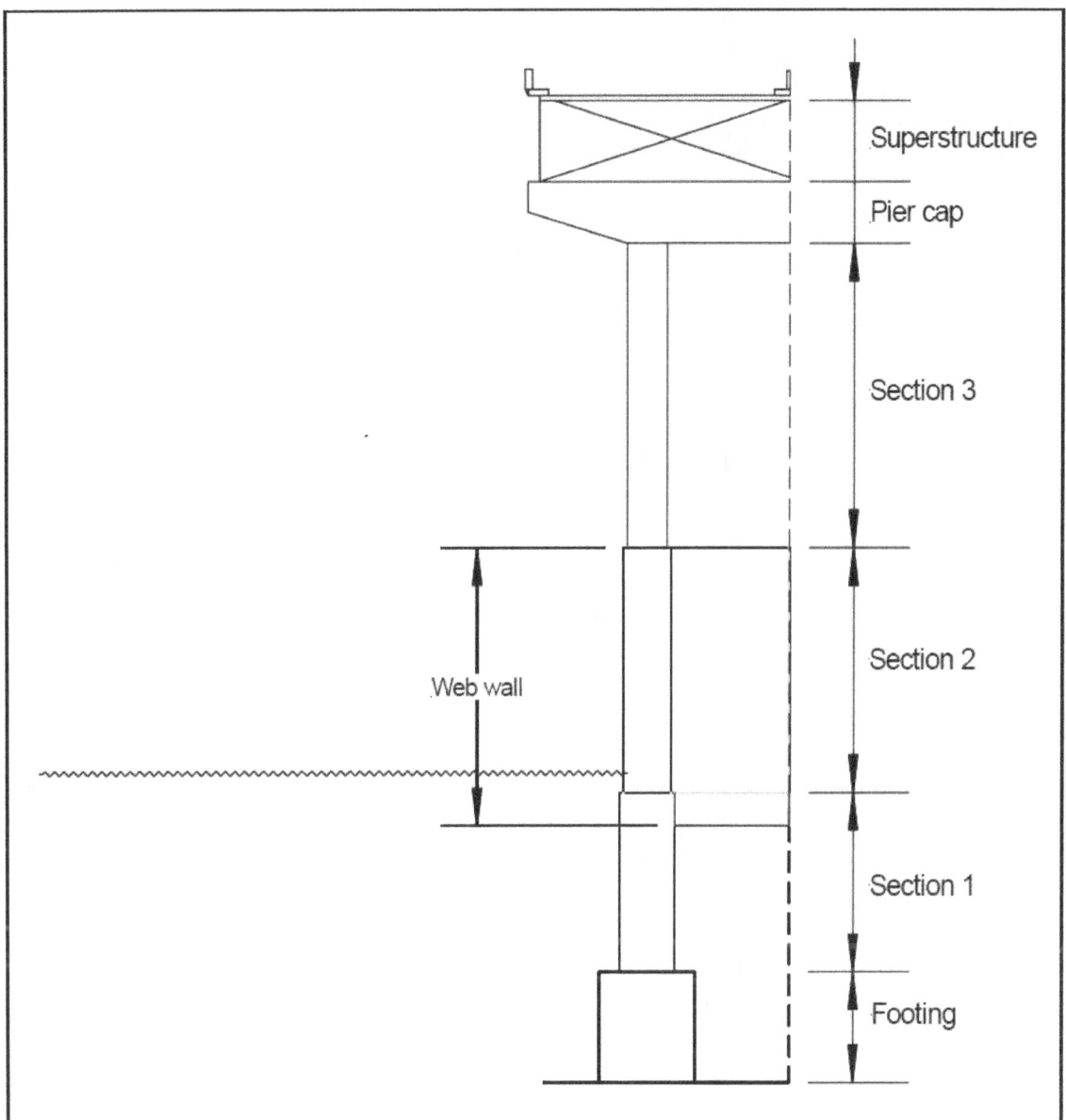

Figure 12. Pier components.

The navigational aids attached to the I-40 bridge consisted of red lights (360 degrees) and red reflectors affixed to the steel girders, marking the location of the main span piers for north and southbound shipping traffic, and green lights and green reflectors, marking the center of the main span. In addition, red navigation lights and red reflectors were affixed to the pier protection cells. At the time of the accident, a green unlighted buoy, located about 0.35 miles from the bridge, marked the upbound, left side of the channel. (See figure 13.) This buoy was placed about 0.05 miles (264 feet) to the left of the recommended sailing line on USACE's waterway chart.

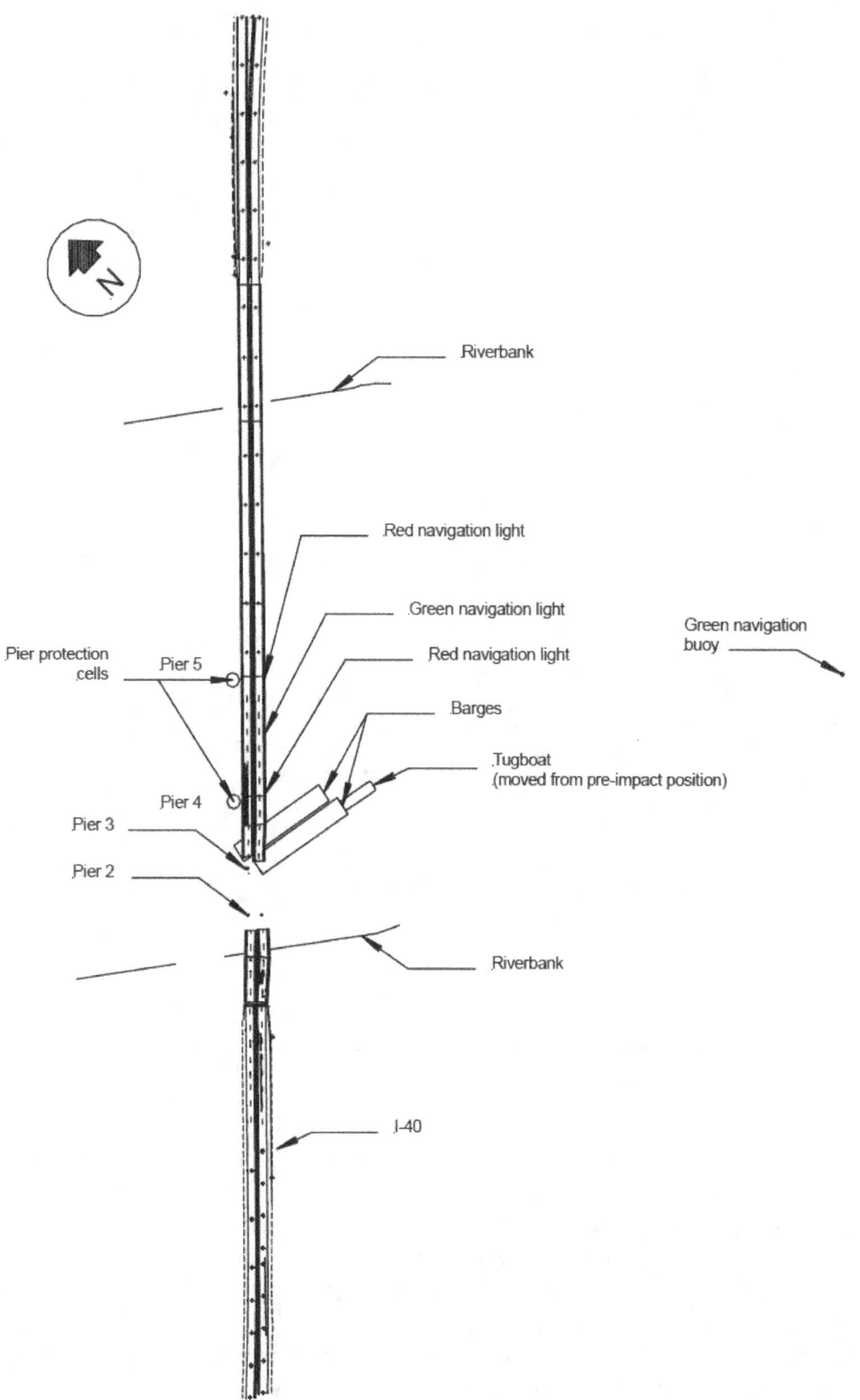

Figure 13. Location of navigational aides on bridge and on upbound channel marker (buoy).

Pier Protection. The channel piers (piers 4 and 5) on the north, or upstream side, of the bridge had protection cells to shield them from vessel impact. (See figures 14 and 15.) The 41.38-foot-diameter pier protection cells had a horizontal clearance, measured at right angles to the axis of the channel, of 296 feet and a top elevation of 476 feet. They consisted of sheet piling driven to bedrock and filled with quarry-run stone from the top of natural ground to the top of the cell. Additional protection consisted of 10-inch by 18-inch by 89-foot-long treated timbers attached to the inside face of piers 4 and 5. No other pier protection systems were installed at the bridge.

Figure 14. Upstream (northern) view of I-40 bridge showing pier protection cells at piers 4 and 5. (Source: ODOT)

Figure 15. Pier protection cell on upstream side of channel pier 5.

According to ODOT, the pier protection system for the main channel was installed in 1984 following previously unreported bridge strikes that resulted in damage that was discovered during bridge maintenance and substructure inspections. Bridge shift detection survey data and maintenance reports indicated that superficial cracks had been observed and recorded on the north (upstream) side of pier 4 during maintenance procedures on September 1, 1977. The report of a subsequent bridge inspection, performed by Blubaugh Engineering Company (BEC) in June 1980 for ODOT, also noted this superficial damage to pier 4 and included comments that this pier had been hit from the north side and had several cracks. BEC recommended that the cracks be filled with an epoxy grout to prevent further deterioration of the pier. Bridge repairs, consisting of structurally rebonding cracks, delaminations, and hollow planes in the Portland cement concrete structures with an epoxy resin (epoxy injection), were completed during repair projects in June 1983 and November 1991 and included piers 2 and 4. ODOT submitted an application to the Coast Guard on November 9, 1982, requesting approval to install pier protection cells at the channel piers of the I-40 bridge, Arkansas Waterway, mile 360.3; construction of the pier protection cells was completed on October 9, 1984.

Before this accident, ODOT did not have a bridge-vessel impact risk assessment program, nor was it required to. As of December 2002, the FHWA's National Bridge Inventory (NBI) recorded 32 bridges in Oklahoma that have navigation controls, meaning that they require a bridge permit (91 percent were built between 1951 and 1990, and 63 percent were built between 1960 and 1970). Since this accident, ODOT has hired a consultant to evaluate bridges at 12 river crossings using the American Association of State Highway and Transportation Officials (AASHTO) *Guide Specification and Commentary for Vessel Collision Design of Highway Bridges*[34] (Vessel Collision Guide Specifications).

Bridge Standards. In the 1960s, when the I-40 bridge was designed and built, lateral load requirements for bridge design followed the 1961 and 1965 editions of the *AASHO*[35] *Standard Specifications for Highway Bridges*. These standards required the following lateral loads to be used in the design of bridge piers: wind loads on the substructure and superstructure, wind loads on the live load (traffic), centrifugal forces from the live load for curved structures, temperature forces, forces from stream current, floating ice and debris, earth pressure as applicable, longitudinal force from the live load, and seismic forces. According to ODOT, except for centrifugal forces and ice floes, the I-40 bridge was designed for the lateral loads specified in the 1961 and 1965 standards. Such loads can produce transverse or longitudinal forces on the piers or a combination of transverse and longitudinal forces. At the time of the allision, lateral load requirements followed the *2002 AASHTO Standard Specifications for Highway Bridges*.[36] None of these standards required that lateral loads caused by vessel impacts be considered.

---

[34] American Association of State Highway and Transportation Officials, *Guide Specification and Commentary for Vessel Collision Design of Highway Bridges* (Washington, DC: AASHTO, 1991).

[35] The American Association of State Highway Officials (AASHO) became AASHTO in the 1970s.

[36] American Association of State Highway and Transportation Officials, *Standard Specifications for Highway Bridges*, 17th ed. (Washington, DC: AASHTO, 2002).

When AASHTO published its Vessel Collision Guide Specifications in 1991, the FHWA recommended their use for bridge design. These specifications recommend probability-based risk analysis and discuss several analytical methods for selecting a design vessel, based upon vessels that typically navigate a waterway. To identify bridges that must continue to function after impact from a design vessel, the specifications recommend classification of bridges as either "critical" or "regular," based on social/survival and security/defense criteria. Critical bridges include transportation routes to essential facilities such as hospitals, police and fire stations, communications centers, and bridges crucial for national defense that are part of the Strategic Highway Network (STRAHNET), including interstate and Federal-aid primary routes. The I-40 bridge would be classified a critical bridge based upon its being part of STRAHNET.

In 1993, AASHTO adopted the load and resistance factor design (LRFD)[37] specifications for new bridges; the LRFD specifications incorporated the 1991 Vessel Collision Guide Specifications. According to the FHWA, the full compliance date for the LRFD is October 2007. (In other words, after October 2007, the LRFD specifications become the official bridge specifications for federally funded bridge construction.) The lateral load requirements in the LRFD include those listed above for the standard specifications and include vehicle and railway collision forces, as well as vessel impact forces.

Experience Using 1991 AASHTO Vessel Collision Guide Specifications in Florida and Louisiana. The NBI lists 551 Florida bridges with navigation controls (72 percent of which were built between 1951 and 1990) and 261 Louisiana bridges with navigation controls (75 percent of which were built between 1951 and 1990). A number of vessel impacts with bridges have occurred in these States, including the ramming of the Sunshine Skyway Bridge by the Liberian tanker *Summit Venture* in Tampa, Florida, in 1980,[38] the striking of the Lake Pontchartrain Causeway in New Orleans, Louisiana, by large tows in 1964,[39] 1974,[40] and 1984,[41] and the striking of the Judge William Seeber Bridge in New Orleans by a tow and empty hopper barge in 1993.[42] Both States currently use the AASHTO Vessel Collision Guide Specifications and the 1994 LRFD specifications.

---

[37] American Association of State Highway and Transportation Officials, *AASHTO LRFD Bridge Design Specifications,* 1st ed. (Washington, DC: AASHTO, 1994).

[38] National Transportation Safety Board, *Ramming of the Sunshine Skyway Bridge by the Liberian Bulk Carrier* Summit Venture, *Tampa Bay, Florida, May 9, 1980,* Marine Accident Report NTSB/MAR-81/03 (Washington, DC: NTSB, 1981).

[39] Tony M. Ducote and Zolan Prucz, "Vessel Collision Vulnerability of Bridges—Louisiana's Role and Perspective," *Proceedings of the 1999 International Bridge Conference* (Pittsburgh, PA: Engineers' Society of Western Pennsylvania, July 1999).

[40] National Transportation Safety Board, safety recommendation letter to the Greater New Orleans Expressway Commission, January 8, 1975, regarding Safety Recommendations H-74-40 through –42, notation 1423.

[41] Ducote and Prucz.

[42] National Transportation Safety Board, *U. S. Towboat* Chris *Collision With the Judge William Seeber Bridge New Orleans, Louisiana, May 28, 1993,* Highway-Marine Accident Report NTSB/HAR-94/03 (Washington, DC: NTSB, 1994).

According to the Florida bridge engineer responsible for bridge-vessel impact risk analysis, for the past 15 years, the Florida Department of Transportation (FDOT) has designed all new bridges over navigable water using the AASHTO Vessel Design Guide Specifications and customized risk analysis software.[43] This software, based upon the AASHTO specification, measures the probability of vessel impact, using vessel data gathered by USACE for all waterways in Florida. The University of Florida's Bridge Software Institute has also developed structural analysis software (FBPier) to determine the plastic structural strength capability of bridge piers subject to vessel impacts. The Florida bridge engineer responsible for vessel impact risk analysis indicated that the average engineering costs to perform vessel impact risk analysis using the structural analysis software should be about the same as those for scour assessments, or approximately $40,000.

In addition, during spring 2004, FDOT measured barge impact forces directly in conjunction with the replacement of the State Route 300-Saint George Island Causeway near Apalachicola, Florida. After the new bridge was open to traffic, Florida test crashed a hopper barge into the older structure at various speeds to obtain direct measurements via instrumentation of the lateral forces imparted to the bridge piers. The purpose of such testing, according to Florida bridge engineers, is to obtain "reliable and accurate barge impact-load data for use in bridge design, retrofit, and evaluation" and to ensure that "the lateral impact loads used for design are effective but do not result in unnecessarily expensive bridge designs."[44] FDOT has completed its physical testing and is analyzing the results. According to the Florida bridge engineer responsible for vessel impact risk analysis, lateral loads computed using the Vessel Collision Guide Specifications can increase the cost of bridge substructures by a factor of 2 to 5.

Louisiana has also developed methods to determine the vulnerability of bridges to vessel impact. In 1984 and 1988, the Louisiana Department of Transportation and Development (Louisiana DOTD) and the FHWA-sponsored research that led to the development of the Vessel Collision Guide Specifications.[45] Later, after the 1993 Judge William Seeber Bridge accident in New Orleans,[46] the Louisiana DOTD started a program to determine the vulnerability to vessel impact of Louisiana bridges over navigable water. The Louisiana DOTD selected 56 of the State's almost 200 bridges over navigable waterways and, working with contractors, examined these bridges to determine the vulnerability to vessel impact and collapse using the criteria in the 1991 Vessel Collision Guide Specifications and the 1994 LRFD bridge specifications. The bridge evaluation found that approximately 50 percent of the bridges examined had vulnerability "above established acceptable risk levels" for main piers, approach bents, and superstructure components. Recommended remedies included both physical protection (pier

---

[43] Vessel Impact Analysis, version 3.05, was developed by the University of Florida for FDOT and is accessible from the FDOT software library <http://www.dot.state.fl.us/structures/proglib.htm>.

[44] Gary Consolazio, Ronald A. Cook, Henry T. Bollman, and J. Darryll Dockstader, "Barge Impacts on Bridges" *TR News 221* (July-August 2002) 29.

[45] Ducote and Prucz.

[46] NTSB/HAR-94/03.

strengthening and pier protection) and preventive measures (installing aids to navigation and limiting the speed of large ships). For instance, the report recommended pier strengthening for one of the channel piers, a two-column bent, of a bridge that crosses the Mississippi River in New Orleans, at an estimated cost of $500,000.

Bridge Management Systems

Bridge management systems (BMSs) are an outgrowth of the NBI and bridge inspection procedures established after the 1967 Silver Bridge collapse[47] and are one of six State management systems once mandated[48] by the Intermodal Surface Transportation Efficiency Act of 1991 (ISTEA). According to AASHTO, a BMS combines management, engineering, and economic inputs to help determine the best actions to take on all bridges in a network over time. A BMS helps engineers and decision makers determine when and where to spend bridge funds so as to "enhance safety, preserve existing infrastructure, and serve commerce and the motoring public."[49]

Bridge Sufficiency Ratings

The FHWA calculates computer-generated bridge sufficiency ratings for all U.S. bridges based on National Bridge Inventory and inspection data submitted by State and local agency bridge inspectors. The sufficiency rating is a numerical rating for a bridge based on its structural adequacy and safety, its serviceability and functional obsolescence, and its essentiality for public use.[50] (See figure 16.) Ratings range from 0 (worst) to 100 (best) and are indicative of a bridge's sufficiency to remain in service. The FHWA uses sufficiency ratings in determining which bridges are eligible for Federal-aid funds. Deficient bridges with sufficiency ratings less than 50 are eligible for complete replacement, and deficient bridges with sufficiency ratings less than 80 are eligible for rehabilitation. The sufficiency rating does not include vulnerability to vessel impact.

The June 2001 sufficiency rating for the I-40 bridge was 67. According to the FHWA's 2001 NBI data, the average age of the 1,177 interstate bridges in Oklahoma is 37 years, and the average sufficiency rating is 76.2. Nationwide, the average age of the 55,263 interstate bridges is 34 years, and the average sufficiency rating is 85.7.

---

[47] National Transportation Safety Board, *Collapse of the U.S. 35 Highway Bridge, Point Pleasant, West Virginia, December 15, 1967,* Highway Accident Report NTSB/HAR-71/01 (Washington, DC: NTSB, 1971).

[48] The use of a formal BMS is now optional, as outlined in 23 CFR Part 500 and as amended by the National Highway System Act of 1995.

[49] American Association of State Highway and Transportation Officials, *Guidelines for Bridge Management Systems* (Washington, DC: AASHTO, 1993) 2.

[50] U.S. Department of Transportation, Federal Highway Administration, *Recording and Coding Guide for the Structure Inventory and Appraisal of the Nation's Bridges,* FHWA-PD-96-001 (Washington, DC: FHWA, 1995) appendix B.

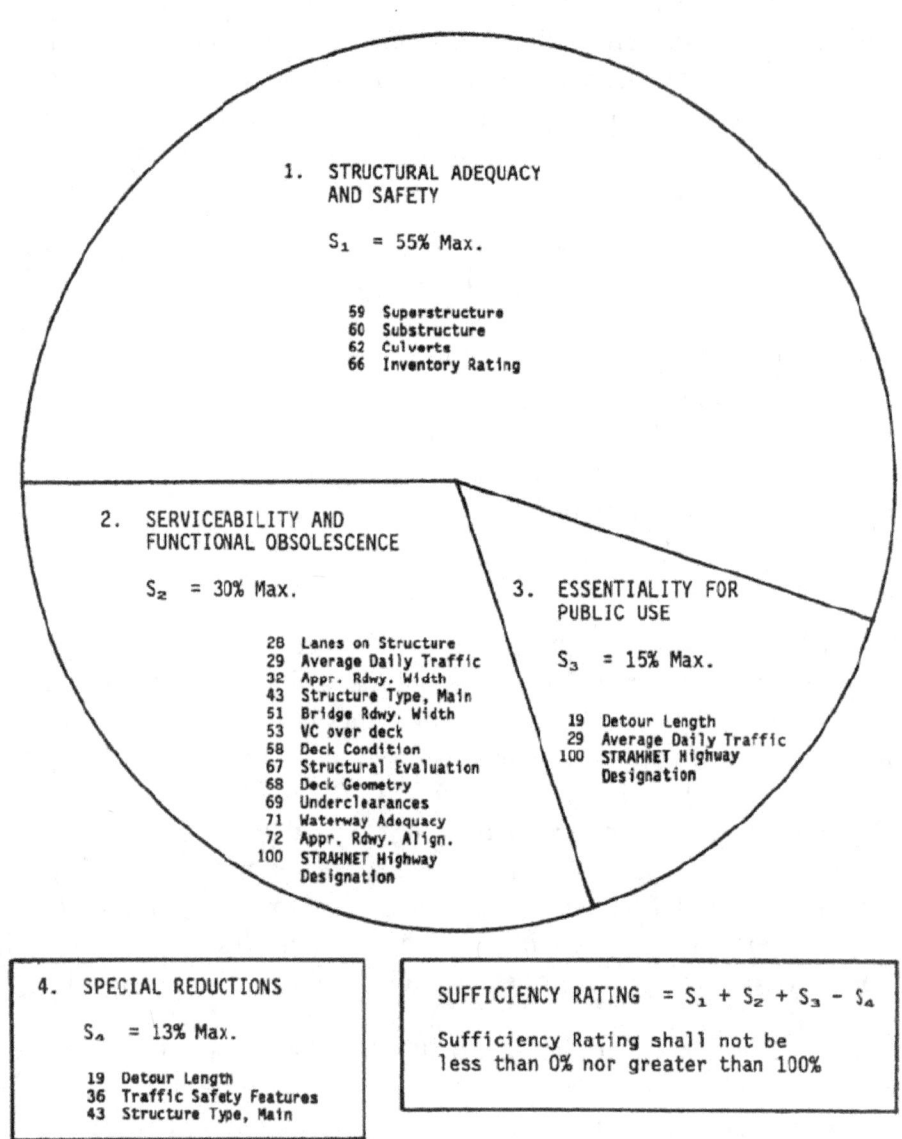

Figure 16. FHWA sufficiency rating factors. (Source: FHWA)

According to ODOT, three bridge inventory items had the most significant effect on the I-40 bridge sufficiency rating: ADT (item 29), substructure (item 60), and bridge roadway width (item 51). Further, according to ODOT, if the ADT (item 29) were reduced to 132 or less, the sufficiency rating could be increased by almost 13 points. If the substructure rating (item 60), which is now 5, were 6 or more, the sufficiency rating would increase by 11 points.[51] Finally, the bridge roadway width (item 51) should equal the approach roadway width. The I-40 bridge is 64 feet wide and the roadway approaching it is 84 feet wide, thereby lowering the bridge's sufficiency rating by 6 points.

---

[51] According to ODOT, the substructure rating was reduced to 5 because of erosion, with undermining of the west abutment, and spalling, with exposed reinforcing, on some of the pier caps.

A bridge inventory item's effect on the sufficiency rating is calculated as a percentage, and its value thus varies depending on the bridge's overall sufficiency rating. For example, if a sufficiency rating is 67, a change in the length of the detour route may change the sufficiency rating by 2.7 points. If a sufficiency rating is 98, the same change in the length of the detour route would affect the sufficiency rating by 0.1 points. Table 5 shows the bridge inventory items that reduced the I-40 bridge's sufficiency rating from 100 to 67.

Table 5. I-40 bridge sufficiency rating reductions.

Bridge inventory item number	Item description	I-40 bridge	Best results	Reduction	Cumulative sufficiency rating
Item 19	Detour length	9 miles	5 miles or less	0.1	99.9
Item 29	ADT	21,610	132 or less	12.9	87.0
Item 51	Bridge roadway width	64 feet	84 feet (roadway width)	6.0	81.0
Item 58	Deck rating	5	7 or more	1.0	80.0
Item 59	Superstructure rating	6	7 or more	0.0	80.0
Item 60	Substructure rating	5	7 or more	11.0	69.0
Item 100	Defense highway designation	STRAHNET	Not STRAHNET	2.0	67.0

Meteorological Information

Observations from the Oklahoma Climatological Survey's Webbers Falls automatic environmental monitoring station 2.2 miles upriver from the accident site showed that at 0745 the air temperature was 64° F, the relative humidity was 92 percent, and the winds were variable at 3 to 5 mph. Sunrise was about 0610. In addition, at 0753, the National Weather Service station at Muskogee Davis Field, about 18 miles northwest of the accident site, reported overcast conditions with surface visibility of 10 miles. According to the captain of the *Robert Y. Love*, the skies were partly cloudy and visibility was clear.

Medical and Pathological Information

Postaccident Toxicology

As required by both 46 CFR 16.240[52] and company policy,[53] toxicological testing was conducted on the captain following the accident. At 1115, a blood sample was taken

---

[52] Title 46 CFR 16.240 requires that the company perform toxicological testing on any crew involved in a "serious marine incident." Title 49 CFR 40.85 specifies the five drugs for which the laboratory tests.

[53] *Vessel Operations Procedures Manual*—Section 4, subsection "Policy," heading "Drug and Alcohol Policy."

from the captain at the Muskogee Immediate Care Clinic and, at the request of Safety Board investigators on scene, a split sample of the blood specimen was sent to the Civil Aerospace Medical Institute (CAMI), Oklahoma City, Oklahoma, for testing. The captain tested negative for the five illicit drugs: marijuana, cocaine, opiates, phencyclidines (PCPs), and amphetamines.[54] Testing results were also negative for benzodiazepines, barbiturates, antidepressants, meprobamate, methaqualone, and nicotine.

At 1345, a urine sample was also collected at the Muskogee Immediate Care Clinic. The samples were sent to the Clinical Reference Laboratory in Lenexa, Kansas, by Federal Express. Testing was negative for marijuana metabolites, cocaine metabolites, phencyclidine, opiates metabolites, and amphetamines. Further, alcohol was not detected in either the captain's blood or urine specimens.

The CAMI testing detected a low level of the antihistamine diphenhydramine[55] in both the captain's blood (0.009 ug/ml) and urine (0.083 ug/ml). The captain stated that he had occasional sinus problems and carried Benadryl® with him for use when needed; he noted he had taken two Benadryl® capsules to treat a sinus headache the night before the accident. The captain stated that he did not drink alcohol and was not taking any prescription medicines at the time of the accident. Inquiries made at pharmacies near the captain's home revealed no prescriptions filled for him in the 90 days before the accident.

Postaccident drug tests were also conducted on the other crewmembers on duty at the time of the allision. Urine samples were taken from the deckhand, the chief engineer, and the mate on May 28, 2002, at 0945, 0950, and 0955, respectively. The samples were tested for the five illicit drugs mentioned earlier in this section; test results were negative. No postaccident alcohol testing was conducted on the other crewmembers, nor was it required because they were not on duty during the accident.

Medical Information

The Safety Board reviewed the captain's preaccident medical records, including Coast Guard medical records, employer medical records, personal medical records, hospital records, pharmacy records, and health insurance records. They revealed treatment for short-term illnesses and injuries, with complete resolution of symptoms.

In 1992, the captain underwent a nonfasting measurement of total cholesterol and triglycerides in conjunction with a Coast Guard-required physical examination for license renewal. The values were elevated, but no additional evaluation of this report was noted. The captain's most recent Coast Guard-required physical examination for license renewal, performed November 3, 1997, indicated no medication use and no abnormal physical findings. The captain stated that he did not have a history of heart or vascular disease, heart surgery, dizziness or fainting, or periods of unconsciousness. The examination form also

---

[54] "Dangerous drugs" are further referenced in the Coast Guard regulations at 46 CFR 4.06-40, 46 CFR 5.35, and 46 CFR 5.59, and are defined at 46 CFR 16.105. The regulations at 46 CFR 113 require testing for marijuana, cocaine, opiates, PCPs, and amphetamines.

[55] An over-the-counter sedating antihistamine commonly used to treat allergic conditions, often known by the trade name Benadryl®.

indicated that the captain's vision was corrected to a visual acuity of 20/20.[56] His field of vision was found to be 180° and his color vision was normal. When asked about his hearing, the captain stated that he had his hearing checked frequently and that he had lost 10 to 15 percent of his hearing. The captain's physical exam found his hearing to be normal.

Following this accident, the captain was admitted to a local regional medical center for examination, observation, and comprehensive medical testing. Heart function was noted to be normal on stress testing and echocardiography. A nuclear medicine imaging study performed in conjunction with the stress test was reported as negative for significant reduction in blood flow.[57] All testing results were essentially normal, except for total occlusion of the mid-left circumflex coronary artery discovered on cardiac catheterization. Later, the captain was admitted to a hospital nearer his home, where he underwent a diagnostic electrophysiology study (EPS),[58] in which serious abnormal heart rhythms were generated, and also underwent subsequent implantation of an implantable cardioverter defibrillator (ICD) because of, according to the captain's cardiologist, his "inducible ventricular flutter[59] with known coronary disease" and "recent syncope."[60] The Safety Board reviewed posthospitalization records prepared by the captain's cardiologist, which showed that the captain's implantable cardioverter defibrillator had not delivered any defibrillation shocks in the 23 months following its implantation. In that time, the defibrillator had recorded two episodes (June 21, 2002, [5 beats] and October 13, 2003, [5 beats]) of nonsustained ventricular tachycardia.[61] In addition, the device recorded four episodes of sustained tachycardia[62] during a 25-minute period on February 23, 2004. The episodes lasted between 22 seconds and 1.6 minutes, and the most rapid average ventricular heart rate for these four episodes was 182 beats per minute. Three of these episodes resulted in the pacemaker function of the device operating in an attempt to reduce the heart rate. The cardiology records did not note any symptoms of dizziness or loss of consciousness.

The captain described his health as good; he reported that he had recently suffered some dizzy spells at home, which he attributed to overexertion from yard work. He also had sustained a dizzy spell and nausea while on board the towboat *Jennie Dehmer* on the

---

[56] 20/20 refers to Snellen acuity, a measure of the ability to identify an object (typically a letter) of a certain size at a specified distance. Visual acuity of 20/20 is considered "normal" vision.

[57] Such imaging, performed in conjunction with stress testing, is highly predictive of both the absence of significant coronary artery disease and a low risk of cardiac death; cardiac catheterization is usually not required. (See R.A. Nishimura, R.J. Gibbons, and A.J. Tajik, "Noninvasive Cardiac Imaging: Echocardiography and Nuclear Cardiology," *Harrison's Principles of Internal Medicine*, 15th ed., eds. E. Braunwald and others [New York: McGraw-Hill, 2001]).

[58] A procedure in which electric stimuli are applied to the inside of the heart to try to cause abnormal heart rhythms.

[59] A serious abnormal heart rhythm caused by the electric stimuli applied during the EPS study noted above.

[60] Syncope is a loss of consciousness resulting from an interruption of blood flow to the brain and refers here to the captain's episode of incapacitation that immediately preceded the accident.

[61] A short series of rapid abnormal heartbeats that does not progress to a continuing abnormal heart rhythm.

[62] An elevated heart rate that persists beyond several seconds. The recorded information from the device was insufficiently detailed to determine whether these episodes represented the serious abnormal rhythm of ventricular tachycardia or some other type of rhythm (including normal heart rate response to stress) that would result in an elevated heart rate.

Wednesday (May 22, 2002) before this accident, while preparing lunch for the crew. He said that after he lay down, his rest was interrupted twice by phone calls. He stated that when called for watch about 1700, he felt "fine."

Survival Aspects

Eleven vehicles carrying 19 occupants either collapsed with or drove off the bridge. Occupant protection use and injuries within each vehicle were as follows:

Vehicle 1—2002 Honda Odyssey EX. The driver's air bag deployed. The 35-year-old male driver sustained fatal blunt trauma injuries. During recovery operations, he was found without the seat belt buckled across his lap. The passenger compartment was extensively crushed and destroyed.

Vehicle 2—2001 Dodge 3500 Pickup Quad Cab. Both front air bags deployed. Two female occupants, one 49 years old and the other 47 years old, drowned. During recovery operations, they were both removed from the severely mangled passenger compartment; their seat belts were not fastened.

Vehicle 3—2001 Dodge Ram 2500 Laramie SLT. Both front air bags deployed. The belted 59-year-old male driver sustained minor injuries. The 58-year-old female passenger drowned. During recovery operations, she was removed from the passenger seat with her seat belt fastened.

Vehicle 4—2001 Dodge Dakota Quad Cab SLT Pickup. Both air bags deployed. The belted 67-year-old male driver sustained serious injuries (compression fractures of the L2 and L3 vertebrae). The belted 68-year-old female passenger sustained serious injuries (a 10th left rib lateral fracture and an upper-right-arm hematoma).

Vehicle 5—1999 Ford Expedition XLT. Both air bags deployed. The 30-year-old male driver, who was found during recovery operations with seat belt unbuckled, drowned. The 29-year-old female passenger, who was removed during recovery operations from the passenger seat with her seat belt fastened, also drowned. A 3-year-old female, reportedly traveling in a car seat, drowned; her body was found floating 50 feet off the river bank, approximately 0.5 mile south of the recovery barge.

Vehicle 6—2001 Volvo Truck. The driver's air bag deployed. The belted 39-year-old male driver drowned.

Vehicle 7—1999 Freightliner Truck Tractor-Semitrailer. The vehicle did not have an air bag. The belted 37-year-old male driver sustained serious injuries (a fractured right ninth rib, multiple abrasions, and facial lacerations and contusions).

Vehicle 8—2002 Chevrolet 1500 Ex-Cab. Vehicle damage prevented investigators from determining whether the air bag deployed. Both the belted 49-year-old male driver and the belted 49-year-old female passenger drowned.

Vehicle 9—2001 Dodge Ram 2500. Both air bags deployed. The 58-year-old male driver, found with the unbuckled seat belt across his body, drowned. The unbelted 57-year-old female passenger also drowned.

Vehicle 10—1997 Ford Crown Victoria. Both front air bags deployed. Both the belted 51-year-old male driver and the belted 50-year-old female passenger drowned.

Vehicle 11—Mack Truck Tractor-Semitrailer ABF. The vehicle did not have an air bag. The belted 62-year-old male driver sustained minor injuries (a nose laceration, bilateral knee abrasions, forearm abrasions, and head and chest blunt trauma).

Tests and Research

Vessel

The vessel's chief engineer stated that he observed the steering system to be operating normally before the accident. Following the accident, Safety Board investigators examined the *Robert Y. Love's* port and starboard steering systems. Investigators tested the system controls from both the wheelhouse control station and the local control station in the steering gear room. The system operated within established parameters; the swing rate for the rudders was approximately 9 seconds for each hydraulic unit operating independently, and the rudders operated over their full range, left and right, without difficulty.

The vessel's chief engineer stated that he observed the propulsion system to be operating normally before the accident. Following the accident, the main propulsion engines were observed to be operating normally at idle conditions; the unstable barge-bridge on-scene situation precluded more thorough examination of the engine control system.

No one noted oil leaking from any of the vessels in the tow. The Coast Guard Gulf Strike Team was on scene until July 13, 2002, monitoring the situation in the event of a pollution incident.

The *Robert Y. Love* was not fitted with a voyage data recorder, nor was it required to be.

Global Positioning System

The navigation global positioning system (GPS) unit (Furuno model GP 31), located in the wheelhouse, was removed from the *Robert Y. Love* and shipped to the Safety Board's Research and Engineering laboratory for extraction of saved track data. The Furuno model GP 31 is a standard, bridge-mounted unit consisting of a display, soft key controls, and a 12-channel receiver. This GPS unit can store latitude and longitude information for 950 predefined waypoints[63] and also define and store information for up to

---

[63] A waypoint is a particular location on a voyage. Waypoint memory is typically used to store locations that have particular significance, such as a landmark or a particular navigational point of reference.

50 routes, each comprising up to 30 predefined waypoints. It can store latitude and longitude information for up to 1,000 track log points in a separate area of memory. The track log data points represent "snapshots" of the current position of the GPS unit, taken and automatically stored at programmable preset intervals.

The GPS unit saved latitude and longitude positions, but not time information. Postaccident activation of the unit revealed that (1) the unit was set to acquire and store track data once every 0.12 miles, (2) data were sent to both serial ports 1 and 2 using version 2 of the National Marine Electronics Association communication protocols, and (3) GPS latitude and longitude information was recorded using the World Geodetic System 1984 (WGS 84) geodetic reference.[64]

Investigators saved, transferred to waypoint memory, and downloaded from the GPS unit 181 plotter track log points, plotting the downloaded track data against both digital and print source maps, including an aerial photograph of the Arkansas River taken by ODOT. They also plotted Coast Guard-supplied latitude and longitude coordinates for the buoys marking the channel onto the ODOT-supplied aerial photograph. (See figure 17.)

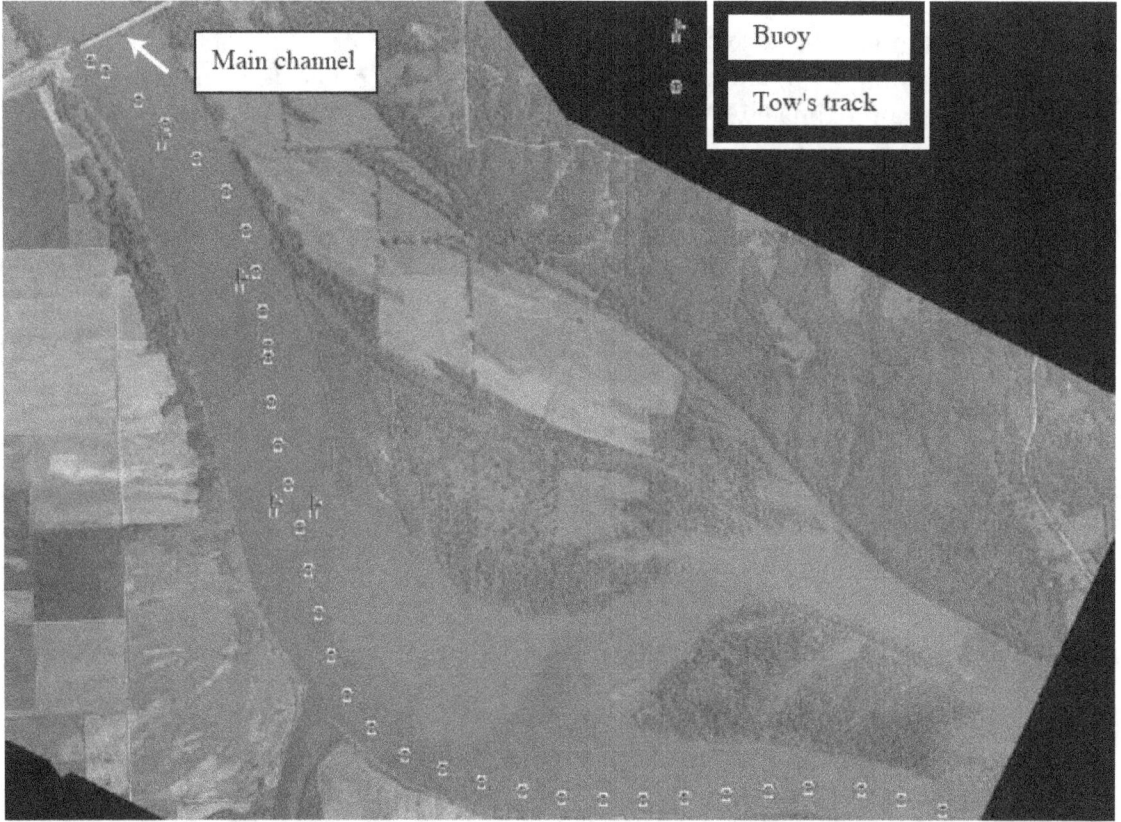

Figure 17. GPS track of the *Robert Y. Love* and tow as plotted on ODOT aerial photograph of upbound approach to I-40 bridge. (Source: Safety Board, with input from ODOT and Coast Guard)

---

[64] WGS 84 is the international standard most commonly used in portable and hand-held GPS navigation units and computer-based mapping software.

Sight Distance

Safety Board investigators interviewed three of the four surviving highway vehicle drivers. They reported traveling at speeds ranging from 57 to 75 mph. Two of the drivers reported vehicles in front of them "disappearing"; both thought the vehicles had driven over the "crown" or "rise" of the bridge. The third driver stated that he was unaware of any bridge problems until he passed over a "rise" and saw that the bridge was out. One of the drivers stated that he applied his brakes, but was unable to stop before driving off the edge.

Safety Board investigators also conducted a physical examination of the roadway, including photographs and videotapes of both the eastbound and westbound approaches to the collapsed bridge section. The videotapes and photographs were taken every 50 feet from eye heights representative of passenger cars (42 inches above the ground) and tractor-semitrailers (94.5 inches above the ground). In addition, accident skid marks in the westbound lanes of I-40 were identified, the longest measuring 170 feet.

The *first point of possible perception* is the first time and place that a hazard can be perceived by a normal, unimpaired driver. After physically examining the approaches to collapsed sections of bridge and reviewing photographs and videotapes, investigators determined the first points of possible perception for the missing bridge section to be as shown in table 6.

Table 6. Sight distances for approaches to void in bridge.

I-40 direction	Vehicle type	Distance (feet)
Eastbound	Passenger	200
Eastbound	Tractor-semitrailer	300
Westbound	Passenger	150
Westbound	Tractor-semitrailer	350

Time Distance

On August 21, 2002, Safety Board investigators recreated the approach to the I-40 bridge in a Coast Guard auxiliary vessel traveling 6.7 mph,[65] which represented the accident vessel's average speed. It took approximately 4 minutes to travel the distance from the upbound channel marker (shown in figure 13) to the bridge.

---

[65] From 0410, the departure time from lock 15 (mile 336.2) until 0745, the time of the allision with the I-40 bridge (mile 360.3), the *Robert Y. Love* and tow averaged 6.7 mph.

Other Information

Licensed Operators' Hours of Service

The hours of service or hours "on watch" per day for the licensed towboat wheelhouse watch personnel (the captain and the pilot) are specified at 46 U.S.C. 8104(h), which states that "an individual licensed to operate a towing vessel may not work for more than 12 hours in a consecutive 24-hour period except in an emergency." A licensed operator on a towing vessel can work any combination of hours, as long as that person is not on watch for more than 12 hours in any 24-hour period.

Not included in the 12-hour work period is standby time, for example, when the vessel is underway, but not moving or waiting to move through a lock or waiting for a tow to be formed. Also not included in the 12-hour work period is the operator's commuting time to a vessel. No regulation or requirement specifies the hours of rest a licensed, uninspected towing vessel operator must have before reporting on board to assume or relieve a watch.

According to MMT, the company complies with the hours-of-service law limiting licensed wheelhouse personnel (captain and pilot) to 12 hours of work in a consecutive 24-hour period. The company does not limit a captain's or pilot's prevoyage commuting distance or time. Inland towing companies normally provide the crew with vehicles to use for their commute, but they do not provide drivers.

Towboat Operator Incapacitation Accidents

The Coast Guard's Accident/Incident Database for 1999 to 2003 contained three towboat accidents in which the towboat operator's incapacitation was identified as the causal factor.

- On February 11, 1999, the pilot of the towboat *Gale C* passed out and the tow became entangled in trees along the bank of the LMR. The unconscious pilot was taken to a hospital; he was later diagnosed with diabetes.

- On November 4, 1999, the pilot of the towboat *Carol P* suffered a stroke. The tow struck a revetment (embankment) on the right bank of the LMR, damaging 2 of 20 loaded barges.

- On March 31, 2003, the pilot of the towboat *Don File* fell from the helm chair and injured the back of his head. As he was lifting himself back into the chair, the chair's arm broke, and he fell to the deck, rendering himself unconscious. The tow and eight barges allided with a small fleet of barges, loaded with stone, at mile 586.2 on the Ohio River.

Alerter Systems

After the I-40 bridge accident, segments of the marine inland towing industry developed alerter systems for use on inland towing vessels. Two systems are being evaluated by the industry. One of the systems continuously monitors steering rudder movements while the tow is underway. It is designed to sound an audible alarm in the wheelhouse if the steering levers are not moved within a given time period. (The systems installed so far use a 2-minute period.) If the captain or pilot on duty does not answer the wheelhouse alarm within 30 seconds, secondary alarms are activated in the captain's and pilot's cabins and in a centrally located crew area. At least one company, American River Transportation Company (ARTCO), has installed this system on all 30 of its line-haul towboats and 30 tug or harbor boats. According to ARTCO, the crews like the system and the wheelmen accept it. As of December 2003, MMT, the owner of the *Robert Y. Love*, had installed the system on five of its towboats and was evaluating its performance for possible installation on the remainder of its fleet. MMT told Safety Board investigators in June 2004 that this system has been installed on its entire fleet of 16 towboats.

A second type of system currently available detects the physical movements of the operator in the wheelhouse. If no movement is detected in the wheelhouse, the system sounds an alarm to alert the crew. The detection system extends no closer than about 2 feet from the deck, so that a person who had collapsed but still was thrashing around on the deck would not prevent the alarm from sounding. At least one major inland towing company, the Kirby Corporation, has installed this system on its towboats; a company representative stated that the system has performed satisfactorily.

American Waterways Operators

The American Waterways Operators (AWO) is a national association representing the inland and coastal tugboat, towboat, and barge industry in the United States. Each year, more than 5,000 tugboats and towboats and more than 25,000 barges carry some 800 million tons of cargo along the Nation's inland and coastal waterways, or about 15 percent of all U.S. freight. The AWO represents about 75 percent of the industry nationwide, which accounts for about 85 percent of the ton-miles of towed traffic. Association members include more than 375 companies and operate more than 25,324 vessels.

In 1994, the AWO instituted a safety management system for its members in the tugboat, towboat, and barge industry known as the Responsible Carrier Program (RCP). The RCP establishes voluntary company safety and environmental protection practices that exceed Government standards in areas that include comprehensive crew training, vessel maintenance procedures, and equipment requirements. Further, the RCP requires that a qualified outside auditor periodically assess the adequacy of the program and the company's compliance. All AWO members must have an approved and active RCP. At the time of the accident, MMT, the owner of the *Robert Y. Love*, had an approved and active RCP and was a member of the AWO.

Coast Guard-AWO Safety Partnership

Allison Work Group. After this accident, the Coast Guard-AWO Safety Partnership[66] convened a working group to determine what could be done to correct problems related to bridge allisions. As part of its research, the group reviewed the Coast

Guard marine accident database for the years 1992 to 2001 to identify bridge allisions involving inland towing vessels and barges. The group found 2,692 bridge allisions involving towing vessels and barges from a tow or breakaway barges, as shown in table 7.

Table 7. Distribution of 2,692 bridge allisions among 559 bridges from 1992 to 2001.

Frequency of allisions	Number of bridges
170	1
91-100	2
81-90	0
71-80	1
61-70	2
51-60	0
41-50	9
31-40	1
21-30	10
11-20	19
10	5
9	7
8	10
7	10
6	14
5	24
4	25
3	45
2	89
1	285

[66] Central to the structure of the Coast Guard-AWO Safety Partnership is the National Quality Steering Committee, which comprises senior Coast Guard and industry leaders <http://www.uscg.mil/hq/gm/nmc/ptp/ptpart/awo.htm>.

Using USACE's latest data for the year 2000, the working group calculated a ratio of 6 bridge allisions for every 10,000 towing vessel trips. It grouped the 2,692 bridge allision accidents into five severity classes, as shown in table 8.

Table 8. Bridge allision severity groups.

Severity class	Number of accidents	Results
0	1,702	No damage
1	610	Damage $1 to $25,000
2	220	Damage $25,001 to $100,000
3	99	Damage $100,001 to $500,000
4	61	Damage over $500,000 or loss of life,* or injury/injuries, missing persons, or oil spilled
*Three of the accidents resulted in fatalities.		

The working group also conducted a statistical analysis of the database, which yielded information about the most frequently hit bridges, the bridges that sustained the most damage, and the bridges scheduled for alteration or removal under the Truman-Hobbs Act.[67] The group found no record of any previous allision with the I-40 bridge. The working group concluded in its report,[68] "Analyses of the allisions by vessel characteristics (e.g., length, horsepower, etc.), time of day of the accident, and occurrence of a pollution incident showed no correlations or patterns suggesting fruitful areas for further study."

Rather than analyze all 2,692 cases individually, the Group opted to examine 473 cases, constituting all of the cases from severity classes 3 and 4 and a random sample from the other severity classes. Of the 473 cases, the working group analyzed causal factors analysis on 459,[69] of which one case cited operator incapacitation as the initiating event for an accident. The resulting analyses indicated that 90 percent of allisions were caused by human performance errors, primarily faulty decision-making; 5 percent, by equipment failures; and 5 percent, by undetermined causes.

In discussing the results of this study with Safety Board staff, the AWO's president stated that the analyses did not show a causal link between the accident data and operator fatigue, manning levels, or the use of over-the-counter medications; the AWO president also stated that he recognized that the data were incomplete with regard to human factors issues. To provide future analysts with more detailed information than was available in most of the cases reviewed by the working group, the working group's report recommended that the Coast Guard implement a special investigative effort for bridge

---

[67] Enacted June 21, 1940, the act, as amended (54 Stat. 497; 33 U.S.C. 511-523), provides authority to the Commandant, U.S. Coast Guard, to alter or remove obstructive bridges across the navigable waters of the United States.

[68] *Report of the U.S. Coast Guard–American Waterways Operators Bridge Allision Work Group*, May 2003.

[69] The group deemed 14 cases unusable for analysis because of missing files or data entry problems.

allision incidents in which the preliminary investigation showed human factors issues as a possible causal factor. The report further recommended that Coast Guard and AWO analysts regularly evaluate the data from these completed investigations and report their findings to the National Quality Steering Committee of the Coast Guard-AWO Safety Partnership. The working group also recommended that the Coast Guard and AWO work jointly to:

- Identify vulnerable bridges requiring measures to prevent and/or mitigate allisions, taking into consideration the costs and benefits of requiring additional protection.

- Develop best practices for transiting bridges vulnerable to allision, and train operators in these practices.

- Require route familiarization, posting,[70] or a check-ride before permitting an operator to navigate alone under a vulnerable bridge.

- Improve Coast Guard-industry information sharing on near-misses.

- Require that the towing industry implement Crew Endurance Management Systems (CEMSs).[71]

- Accelerate the removal and alteration of "unreasonably obstructive" bridges under the authority of the Truman-Hobbs Act.[72] The working group's report noted, "More than 900 bridge allisions—34 percent of all allisions between 1992-2001—occurred at bridges under order to be altered or on the Truman-Hobbs backlog priority list."

The working group also recommended that the Coast Guard Research and Development Center use this report as a basis for future studies on synergistic combinations of actions resulting from the recommendations above.

---

[70] Western River term for the process of familiarizing a licensed pilot with specific sections of a river under the supervision of an experienced, licensed pilot. Once a pilot is considered qualified to navigate a section of river, he or she is considered "posted."

[71] This process, derived from the CEMS originally developed for the Army Safety Center in the early 1990s, allows companies to produce work and rest management plans that optimize alertness and performance during duty hours and subsequently develop a crew endurance plan that meets their specific needs. The CEMS coordinates a network of interrelated factors such as (1) company mission (for example, provide transport for oil companies); (2) equipment limitations (for example, type of vessel, and onboard crew facilities); (3) environmental factors (for example, voyage duration, noise, and light levels); (4) crewmembers' physiological and psychological limitations; and (5) crew rest and work hours policies.

[72] This authority is delegated to the Commandant of the U.S. Coast Guard. The Commandant, represented by the Chief, Office of Bridge Administration (G-OPT), manages the alteration program for unreasonably obstructive bridges, including providing planning, programming, and budgeting; legal interpretations; and technical engineering assistance. The laws relating to unreasonably obstructive bridges across the navigable waters of the United States are contained in the following statutes: (1) The Rivers and Harbors Appropriations Act of 1899, section 18 (30 Stat. 1153; 33 U.S.C. 502); (2) The Bridge Act of 1906, sections 4 and 5 (34 Stat. 85; 33 U.S.C. 494-495); and (3) The Act of June 21, 1940, as amended (Truman-Hobbs Act), (54 Stat. 497; 33 U.S.C. 511-523).

Recent Developments. In November 2003, the AWO held a joint meeting of the AWO Interregion and Coastal Safety Committees in Baltimore, Maryland. At this meeting, participants discussed safety issues that affect the marine towing industry, such as the safety of bridge transits and towing vessel operator incapacitation.

Discussions during the joint meeting of these safety committees indicated that inland marine training facilities in Houston, Texas, and Paducah, Kentucky, have incorporated incapacitation scenarios in their towboat crewmember training simulations. In addition, the AWO safety committees have developed procedures for inclusion in RCP practices concerning operator incapacitation and bridge transit procedures. These procedures include provisions for on-duty personnel to check the wheelhouse hourly, or before navigating through bridges or through restricted or narrow channels, to ensure that the wheelman is alert and in control of the vessel; they also contain actions to be taken when a wheelman is found incapacitated. The AWO Board has not yet taken an official position on the wheelhouse monitoring and bridge transit procedures; its evaluation is ongoing.

Crew endurance management, which provides the ability to maintain performance within safety limits while enduring job-related physical, psychological, and environmental challenges. CEMS demonstration projects are underway in at least eight companies and on 40 towing vessels, and 150 CEMS "coaches" have been trained, according to the AWO. In addition, the Coast Guard has, for a number of years, been working with the towing industry, through the AWO and its member companies, in demonstration project(s) using CEMSs on towing vessels. This project aims to develop a system for managing the risk factors that can lead to human error and performance degradation in maritime work environments. One goal of this project is to ensure sufficient hours of uninterrupted sleep for watchstanders within the existing hours of duty.

The Coast Guard is now required to report to Congress on CEMS initiatives. On August 9, 2004, the Coast Guard and Maritime Transportation Act of 2004 became Public Law 108-293, which amends section 409, "Hours of Service on Towing Vessels" as follows:

> (b) Demonstration Project. Prior to prescribing regulations under this section the Secretary shall conduct and report to the Congress on the results of a demonstration project involving the implementation of Crew Endurance Management Systems on towing vessels. The report shall include a description of the public and private sector resources needed to enable implementation of Crew Endurance Management Systems on all United States-flag towing vessels.

Motorist Warning Systems

About 0210 on September 15, 2001, the towboat *Brown Water V*, pushing four barges,[73] struck the Queen Isabella Causeway, which connects South Padre Island to the mainland in Cameron County, Texas.[74] The allision caused two spans of the 2.37-mile-long causeway to collapse. Ten passenger vehicles either fell with the collapsing sections or drove off the end of the remaining roadway structure, resulting in eight fatalities. A third adjacent section of the bridge collapsed later that day. Bridge repair costs totaled approximately $14.2 million, including $2.3 for demolition, $4.8 million for reconstruction, and $7.1 million for ferries to provide temporary transportation.

Weather conditions reported at 0210 by Brownsville International Airport, 18 miles southwest of the accident site, were as follows: 7 miles of visibility, temperature 74° F, peak wind gusts out of the south-southeast (160°T) at 18.2 knots (21 mph), no precipitation, and clear skies. According to the Coast Guard, the water current across the flats of the Laguna Madre Bay was approximately 4 to 5 mph, running from the southeast toward the northwest, almost in line with the channel.

The collapsed causeway, with a 2001 ADT of 23,069, was the only vehicular link from South Padre Island to the mainland. Opened to traffic in 1974, it was constructed solely with State funds and spanned the Laguna Bay at the Gulf Intercoastal Waterway at mile marker 667.4 at Port Isabel, Texas. The main channel span, at piers 35 and 36, had a horizontal clearance of 275 feet between the fender systems and a vertical clearance of 73 feet. The channel piers had pier protection. The tow struck the unprotected pier 32, 175 feet west of the channel. (See figures 18A and 18B.)

---

[73] The barges had a draft of approximately 9 feet, the overall length of the tow was 851.1 feet, and the combined weight of the vessels and their cargo was 9,030.9 tons. The *Brown Water V* was propelled by 600 horsepower.

[74] NTSB docket number HWY-01-I-H036.

Figure 18A. Channel piers and damaged piers and collapsed section.

Figure 18B. Pier protection on east channel pier.

After the 2001 accident, the Texas Department of Transportation installed an early warning collapse detection system. The $850,000 system, which became operational in March 2004, consists of fiber-optic cable, "STOP WHEN FLASHING, DANGER" warning signs, red flashing signals placed every 500 feet along the bridge in both directions, and gates at both ends of the causeway. If the cable is severed, the signals located before the break are designed to flash red, and the signals beyond the break are designed not to flash, allowing traffic to clear the bridge. In addition, the system is to automatically place calls to law enforcement agencies and the Coast Guard.

Lake Pontchartrain Causeway, New Orleans, Louisiana. The Lake Pontchartrain Causeway in New Orleans, Louisiana, has a motorist information/warning system, operated by the Greater New Orleans Expressway Commission, consisting of a marine radar system that scans the lake for targets, warning the bascule bridge operators if a vessel is within 1 mile of the bridge (prohibited zone). According to the Commission, bridge operators can contact the vessel by marine radio and, if necessary, activate the hazard incident lighting system yellow flashers spaced every 4/10 mile for the length of the 24-mile bridge. Variable message signs are placed every 3 miles at the crossovers. The system is used to warn motorists of accidents on the bridge as well as potential bridge span failures.

Police dispatch personnel, who also monitor marine frequencies and post warning messages on the variable message signs, are notified of any incident. If a potential threat to the bridge structure exists, traffic is stopped at the toll plazas and the drawbridge (16-mile marker). Police units are dispatched to the projected impact area to close the lanes in both directions. The Coast Guard is notified for enforcement action in the prohibited zone.

Sunshine Skyway Bridge, Tampa Bay, Florida. The Sunshine Skyway Bridge in Tampa Bay, Florida, has a motorist warning system that consists of digital message signs to warn motorists of high winds on the bridge. No other types of motorist advisory systems currently operate on the bridge. According to FDOT, the Sunshine Skyway Bridge has a continuity warning system that would advise FDOT and the highway patrol of a major discontinuity in the bridge. FDOT characterized this system as being less than totally dependable.

Technical Guidance. On February 11, 1983, the FHWA issued Technical Advisory T5140.19, "Pier Protection and Warning Systems for Bridges Subject to Ship Collisions." Although this advisory and the Vessel Collision Guide Specifications describe motorist warning systems, neither document provides guidance on their use.

Related Bridge Sensor Research. Alabama A&M University, using nanotechnology, has designed fiber-optic sensors for concrete overpasses and bridges that can alert engineers to stresses and damage caused by loads and weather. In addition, West Virginia University has equipped the 1,000-foot Star City Bridge over the Monongahela River near Morgantown, West Virginia, with finely tuned sensors to measure minuscule, visually undetectable changes in steel girders and support structures, in piers and abutments, and in concrete and reinforcing bars. In addition, New Mexico State University researchers have embedded optical sensors in an I-10 overpass in Las Cruces, New Mexico, and in an I-40 bridge over Rio Puerco west of Albuquerque, New Mexico, to measure stress and strain in the concrete beams.

According to the FHWA, recent research on short-term monitoring instrumentation has been successful, and the agency is working to improve the ability of long-term monitoring instrumentation to withstand weather conditions.[75] The FHWA further notes that, as part of the Structural Health Monitoring (SHM) approach to obtaining quantitative information for efficient infrastructure assessment and management, research in recent years has focused on moving from traditional bridge inspection methodologies relying on visual inspection to the application of sensing technology. In March 2004, the FHWA established a "Virtual Team for Structural Health Monitoring," consisting of FHWA bridge engineers and representatives from State highway agencies, academia, and industry, to advance SHM.

Bridge Safety and Security

After the September 11, 2001, terrorist attacks in the United States, the National Cooperative Highway Research Program and the AASHTO Task Force on Transportation Security developed *A Guide to Highway Vulnerability Assessment for Critical Asset Identification and Protection.*[76] Some of the guide's proposed countermeasures for bridge protection include built-in monitors on bridges, cameras for surveillance, motion sensors or other active devices, column protection, advance warning systems, and barriers around bridge piers.

In September 2003, the FHWA/AASHTO Blue Ribbon Panel on Bridge and Tunnel Security completed another study, *Recommendations for Bridge and Tunnel Security*, requested by the AASHTO Task Force on Transportation Security. It discusses eight types of threats: low-tech and high-tech conventional explosives, for example, shape charges; explosively formed penetrating devices, such as kinetic energy penetrators; low-tech, hand-held cutting devices; truck- or barge-size conventional explosives; chemical or biological agents released in tunnels; incendiary conventional explosives; hazardous materials releases in tunnels; and intentional ramming by ship or barge.

---

[75] March 17, 2004, telephone conversation with FHWA bridge engineers.

[76] *A Guide to Highway Vulnerability Assessment for Critical Asset Identification and Protection*, National Cooperative Highway Research Program Project 20-07/Task 151B (Vienna, VA: Science Applications International Corporation, Transportation Policy and Analysis Center, May 2002).

In a recent white paper, "Bridges for the 21st Century, Focus Area Bridge Safety, Reliability and Security," the FHWA states:

> It is common knowledge that our bridges are deteriorating at a faster rate than we can fix them...there simply aren't enough resources to continue conducting business as usual...it is essential to develop innovative, revolutionary solutions to rebuild our infrastructure. The goal...is to ensure safety of bridges and structures against all manmade and natural hazards....A research program needs to be implemented which develops breakthrough innovations, new structural systems and rapid construction/reconstruction practices and systems that become the standard, and produces long-lived facilities to counteract the effects of earthquakes, scour, wind, overloads, collisions, and terrorist attacks.

The paper discusses natural threats to bridges, such as seismic events, hydraulics and hydrology, and wind, and manmade threats to bridges, such as terrorist acts, bridge overloads, vessel impacts, and fire. The paper also notes: "The most vulnerable locations for major damage to a bridge over water are the piers. Our code does not consider carefully enough collisions with barges and other commercial or enemy craft."

Analysis

General

This analysis first identifies the factors and conditions that the Safety Board was able to exclude as neither causing nor contributing to the accident. It then provides a brief overview of the accident events, followed by a detailed discussion of these major safety issues: the captain's incapacitation and countermeasures for such an event; bridge protection, including risk assessment; and mitigation of loss of life, including motorist warning systems.

Exclusions

The captain of the *Robert Y. Love* was tested for alcohol and illegal drugs about 3.5 hours after the allision, and the results for both were negative. The captain had held an uninspected towing vessel operator's license for almost 30 years, had extensive towing experience on the inland waters of the United States, and was familiar with the accident area. The weather was mild, river conditions were calm, and skies were clear. The barge tow was small, the barges were empty, and no external forces or conditions, such as high winds, rain, fog, or high current, were present that would have increased the captain's workload in controlling the movement of the tow. The river's contour for lining up the tow to pass through the navigation span of the bridge did not require excessive maneuvering; further, the relatively wide navigation span (296 feet), the barge tow's width of 108 feet, and the 2-mph current conditions would have made for an uncomplicated passage through the navigation span.

The towboat had sufficient horsepower for control of the barge tow. Postaccident inspection of the towboat revealed no mechanical anomalies that would have caused the tow to veer off course from the navigation channel. Fishing tournament witnesses immediately rescued vehicle occupants in the water, and the first of 58 local, State, and Federal agencies responded in 8 minutes. The Safety Board therefore concludes that the captain was not impaired due to alcohol or illegal drugs. Further, neither the weather nor the mechanical condition of the towboat nor the captain's qualifications, experience, familiarity with the river, or workload contributed to the accident. Finally, the emergency response was adequate and timely.

The Safety Board examined the captain's 72-hour history to determine whether fatigue was a factor in his incapacitation before the tow struck the bridge. In the 3 days before the accident, the captain experienced significant disruption to his work-related sleep patterns. On May 24, 2002, he reduced his normal (6-hour) afternoon sleep by 3 hours. The captain remained awake during the night of May 24 and into the morning of May 25, completely missing one sleep period. On the morning of May 25, the captain went to bed at the time he would normally be waking up and slept for 4 hours. In addition, he shared driving an automobile with another person for approximately 10 hours while traveling to meet the *Robert Y. Love*, remaining awake through his entire afternoon sleep period. Assuming an average of 5.5 hours of sleep obtained during each off-watch period, the captain's unusual sleep patterns in 72 hours before the accident resulted in a sleep debt of about 10 to 11.5 hours.

Research has shown that sleep loss compromises daytime functions; virtually everyone experiences reduced performance efficiency when not sleeping adequately.[77] Even modest sleep reduction, as little as 1 hour per night, can accumulate over time, progressively increasing daytime sleepiness.[78] Also, small reductions in sleep, as little as 2 hours, can result in measurable changes in vigilance.[79] The Safety Board determined, based on the captain's altered sleep pattern in the 72 hours before the accident, that although the captain had complied with both company policy and Federal regulations regarding hours of service, he was sleep-deficient at the time of the accident.

The captain had been working (on duty on board the vessel) for only about 6 of the 24 hours immediately preceding the accident. He had stood watch the evening before and slept for at least 5 hours before going on watch the morning of the accident. However, although the captain had slept before the accident, the amount of sleep that he received was insufficient to compensate for the deficit incurred while traveling, and he was therefore sleep-deficient. When examining the circumstances of the captain's loss of consciousness, investigators relied heavily on his statements, notably that his loss of consciousness occurred "all at once." His last recollection before the allision was preparing for passage under the bridge. He described being out of his chair, crouched on the floor, and below the level of the vessel control console upon regaining consciousness and further stated that he had trouble with his vision and could not "get oriented right." The captain's description of his loss of consciousness and recovery are atypical of a fatigue or "falling asleep" incident. Additional factors, such as his recent conversation with the deckhand and the time of day also argue against falling asleep. Therefore, the Safety Board concludes that the captain's incapacitation was probably not a result of his falling asleep.

The captain said he had taken Benadryl® the evening before the accident, more than 8 hours before the accident occurred. The very low levels of the medication detected in the captain's blood following the accident are consistent with his statements. Diphenhydramine (commonly known by the trade name Benadryl®) is an over-the-counter

---

[77] Meir H. Kryger, Thomas Roth, and William C. Dement, eds., *Principles and Practice of Sleep Medicine*, 2nd ed. (Philadelphia: W.B. Saunders Company, 1994).

[78] W.C. Dement and C. Fisher, "Experimental Interference With the Sleep Cycle," *Canadian Psychiatric Association Journal* Vol. 8 (1963): 400-405.

[79] (a) R.T. Wilkinson, R.S. Edwards, and E. Haines, "Performance Following a Night of Reduced Sleep," *Psychonomic Science* Vol. 5 (1966): 471-472; (b) D.F. Dinges, F. Pack, K. Williams, K.A. Gillen, J.W Powell, G.E. Ott, C. Aptowicz, and A.I. Pack, "Cumulative Sleepiness, Mood, Disturbance, and Psychomotor Vigilance Performance Decrements During a Week of Sleep Restricted to 4-5 Hours per Night," *Sleep*, 20(4) 1997: 267-277; and (c) T. Roehrs, E. Burduvali, A. Bonahoom, C. Drake, and T. Roth "Ethanol and Sleep Loss: A Dose' Comparison of Impairing Effects," *Sleep*, 26(8) 2003: 981-985.

antihistamine with sedative effects, often used to treat allergy symptoms. In over-the-counter doses, the medication commonly results in drowsiness and has measurable effects on performance of complex cognitive and motor tasks. Reduced performance has been demonstrated even in individuals who report feeling normal after taking the drug.[80] Regular use results in some tolerance to the sedative effects of the medication, though certain performance decrements persist. Studies have reported significant subjective sedation 6 hours following a maximal over-the-counter dose of diphenhydramine[81] and significant reduction in sleep latency (the time it takes to fall asleep in a quiet environment) for at least 7 hours following a maximal over-the-counter dose of diphenhydramine.[82] However, the concentration of diphenhydramine in the blood of the towboat captain was much less than the average concentrations reported in the latter study, consistent with taking a less-than-maximal dose of the medication (depending on the specific preparation, the amount of diphenhydramine contained in a single capsule or tablet could be 12.5 or 25 mg). At least one other study suggests that sedation would be unlikely at this blood concentration.[83]

The Safety Board concludes that although the captain's performance may have been subtly impaired by the low level of diphenhydramine in his blood, and he may have been more prone to falling asleep as a result of taking the medication, neither factor was likely to have accounted for his incapacitation.

The Accident

The *Robert Y. Love* was traveling on the M-KARNS waterway to Catoosa, Oklahoma, with two empty barges when the tow struck the I-40 bridge. The captain was alone on watch in the wheelhouse, navigating the 1274.5-long ton tow at an average speed of 6.7 mph. The captain told investigators that the last thing he remembered was passing the buoy to port and using "a few degrees" of left rudder to align his tow through the main navigation span of the bridge. At 6.7 mph, the Safety Board estimated the transit time from the buoy to the bridge to be about 4 minutes.

---

[80] See, for example, John M. Weiler M.D. and others, "Effects of Fexofenadine, Diphenhydramine, and Alcohol on Driving Performance," *Annals of Internal Medicine* (2000) 132: 354-363, in which the effect 2.5 hours after a 50-mg dose of diphenhydramine is noted to be worse than the effect of an 0.10 blood alcohol level.

[81] J.R. Glass, B.A. Sproule, N. Herrmann, D. Streiner, and U.E. Busto. "Acute Pharmacological Effects of Temazepam, Diphenhydramine, and Valerian in Healthy Elderly Subjects," *Journal of Clinical Psychopharmacology* (June 2003) 23(3): 260-268.

[82] T. Roehrs, A. Zwyghuizen-Doorenbos, and T. Roth, "Sedative Effects And Plasma Concentrations Following Single Doses Of Triazolam, Diphenhydramine, Ethanol and Placebo," *Sleep* 16(4) 2003: 301-305.

[83] S.G. Carruthers, D.W. Shoeman, C.E. Hignite, and D.L. Azarnoff, "Correlation Between Plasma Diphenhydramine Level and Sedative and Antihistamine Effects," *Clinical Pharmacology and Therapeutics* (April 1978) 23(4): 375-382.

Captain's Incapacitation

The captain described an episode of sudden loss of consciousness lasting several minutes, in which he fell, but not completely, because of the limited space between the vessel control console and the deck. He regained consciousness slowly, and remained confused for a short period of time after regaining consciousness. Such an incident is entirely consistent with an episode of syncope, in which blood flow to the brain is interrupted for any of a variety of reasons. This interruption results in loss of consciousness and falling. Normally, after such a fall, an individual is in the horizontal position, allowing blood to flow to the brain and recovery to occur quite rapidly. However, the captain was supported in a crouched position as a result of the limited space in which to fall, and this position did not permit an immediate return of blood flow to his brain. Extensive postaccident testing did not reveal an obvious cause for the captain's loss of consciousness, though the finding of coronary artery disease on cardiac catheterization (without any impairment of heart function) led physicians to recommend an EPS, in which electric stimuli are applied to the inside of the heart to try to cause abnormal heart rhythms. Serious abnormal rhythms were generated, and on the basis of the captain's loss of consciousness that led to the accident, the presence of coronary artery disease, and an abnormal EPS, the captain's cardiologist recommended that an ICD be placed in the captain. It is notable in this case, however, that invasive studies (cardiac catheterization, and EPS) were pursued despite a negative noninvasive evaluation. In particular, given the captain's normal nuclear medicine stress test, it would not have been unusual to forgo invasive cardiovascular testing in a typical clinical setting. Had the captain undergone the noninvasive studies without a history of loss of consciousness, invasive testing almost certainly would not have been pursued.

A prolonged serious abnormal heart rhythm can result in an episode of syncope. However, despite several short episodes of abnormal heart rhythms recorded by his ICD since implantation, the captain has not had any further episodes of syncope nor required any shocks from the device. Syncope can have causes other than abnormal heart rhythms. Examples include vasovagal syncope (the common faint); postural hypotension (when rising too quickly); carotid sinus hypersensitivity (in response to pressure on an area of the neck); heart attack, congestive heart failure and other heart problems; and certain types of migraines. However, no evidence conclusively indicates that any one of these mechanisms actually caused the captain's episode, and, notably, in as many as 50 percent of cases, no specific cause of syncope can be identified.[84] Although the captain had a few short episodes of mild dizziness on occasion before the accident, he not unreasonably attributed these episodes to overexertion, did not suffer any lasting ill effects, and did not report any loss of consciousness, near-loss of consciousness, or any other symptoms that could be attributed to the typical causes of syncope. These episodes were apparently not noteworthy enough for the captain to seek medical attention.

The Safety Board therefore concludes that the captain experienced a sudden loss of consciousness, possibly as the result of an abnormal heart rhythm. The Safety Board also

---

[84] V.M. Voge, J.D. Hastings, and W.E. Drew, "Convulsive Syncope in the Aviation Environment," *Aviation, Space, and Environmental Medicine* (December 1995) 66(12):1198-204.

concludes that the captain had no apparent symptoms of clinical significance prior to the accident, and a reasonable clinical evaluation of the captain before the accident was unlikely to have detected the medical conditions that were discovered through postaccident testing.

The Allision

After the captain's incapacitation, the vessel continued in a left turn and struck pier 3, about 201 feet west of the navigation channel, at an approximately 56-degree angle. (See figure 19.) The Safety Board calculated the kinetic energy of the tow to be 4,498.79 kip-ft (1,000 foot-pounds). (See appendix B for detailed calculations.) Pier 3 was not, nor was it required to be, designed to withstand a concentrated horizontal load of that magnitude,[85] and therefore collapsed. The spans on either side of pier 3 collapsed with it, damaging pier 2 and causing the west column and web wall to collapse. (See figure 20.) In total, 503 feet of bridge deck fell into the river and onto the barges.

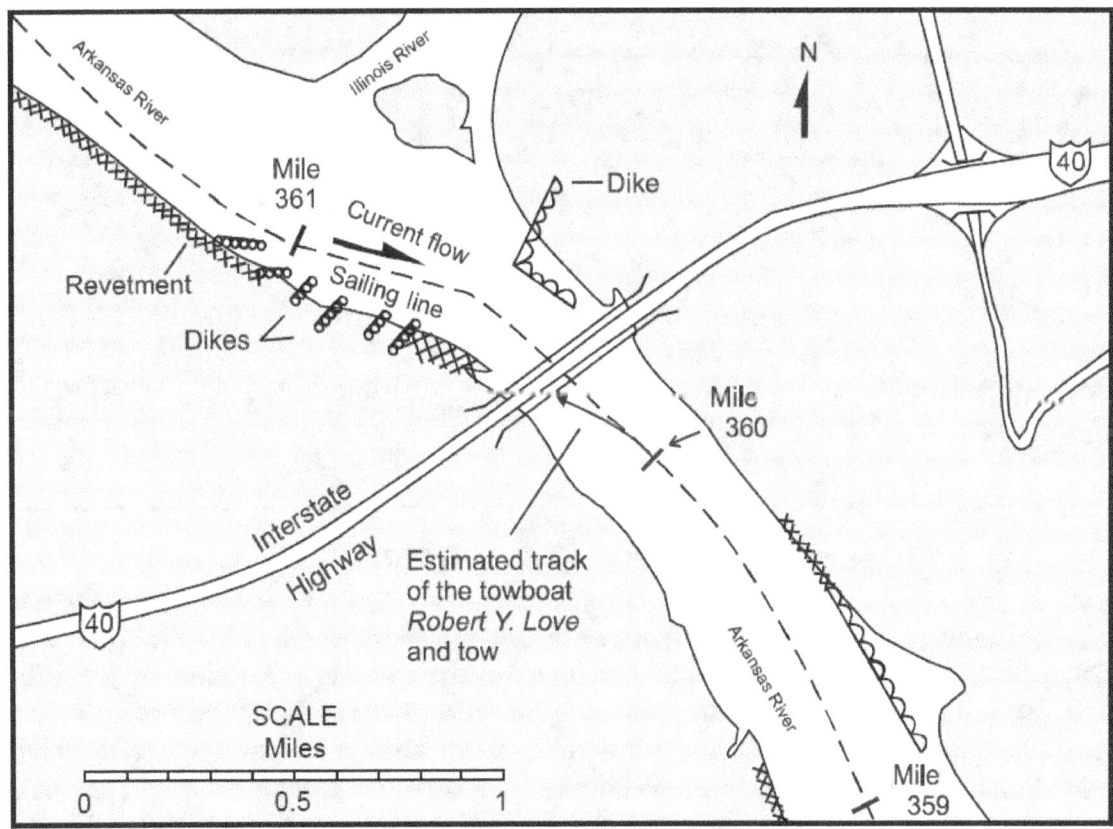

Figure 19. Estimated track of towboat *Robert Y. Love* as it approached I-40 highway bridge.

---

[85] Except for centrifugal forces and ice floes, the I-40 bridge was designed for the lateral loads specified in the 1961 and 1965 standards. For further information, see "Bridge Standards" under *Bridge Information* in the *Highway Information* section of this report.

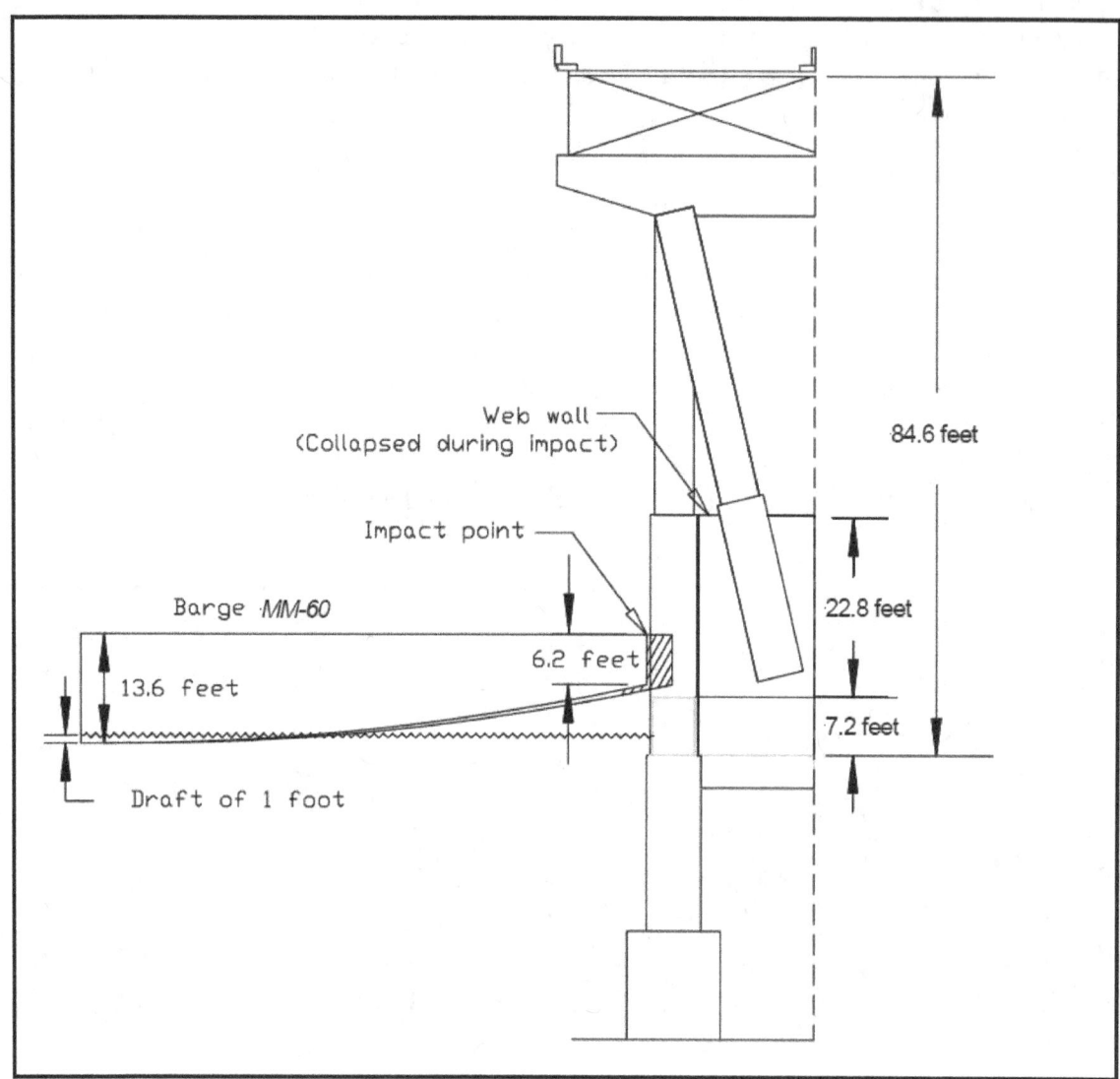

Figure 20. Impact of barge *MM-60* with south column of pier 3.

Highway traffic continued to drive off the bridge into the void after the bridge deck collapsed. A participant in the nearby fishing tournament observed a section of the bridge collapse and several vehicles enter the water. He called 911 and fired a flare from a hand-held flare pistol toward the bridge in front of a tractor-semitrailer traveling westbound to warn the driver of the danger. The truckdriver stopped before reaching the edge, partially jackknifing his truck and blocking the bridge to following highway traffic. By the time roadway traffic had stopped, eight passenger vehicles and three tractor-semitrailer truck combinations had fallen into the river or onto collapsed portions of bridge span. The Safety Board concludes that the quick-acting fisherman who fired the warning flare to alert motorists on the bridge probably prevented further loss of life.

Allision Prevention

Wheelhouse Alerter Systems

In this accident, the captain of the *Robert Y. Love* was incapacitated as the result of an unforeseen medical event. When he lost consciousness, he was alone in the wheelhouse, a not atypical condition aboard U.S. inland towing vessels. The deckhand on duty had just departed the wheelhouse and gone below deck to awaken the mate for duty and to perform routine maintenance tasks. At the time of the accident, the mate had just been awakened, and the engineer was making his rounds of the engineroom. Thus, although three other crewmembers were awake and moving about the vessel in the minutes before the accident, none of them were in the wheelhouse when the captain lost consciousness. The Safety Board estimates the captain became incapacitated about 4 minutes before the impact with the bridge.[86] Had a method been available to alert crewmembers to the problem in the wheelhouse, they could have investigated and possibly taken action that might have prevented the accident.

Since this accident, segments of the marine inland towing industry have been evaluating wheelhouse alerter systems for use on inland towing vessels. These systems, which have already been installed on some towing vessels, are designed to sound an alarm should the vessel operator either fail to move the rudder or fail to physically move for a predetermined period of time. The lack of such movements would indicate the strong possibility that the operator is, for some reason, incapable of making them and would summon assistance to the wheelhouse to investigate the cause.

If the *Robert Y. Love* had been equipped with such a system on the day of the accident, other crewmembers on board the vessel may have been alerted to a problem in the wheelhouse and may have been able to prevent this accident. Therefore, the Safety Board concludes that the presence of either another crewmember in the wheelhouse or a wheelhouse alerter system might have resulted in timely action that could have prevented this accident.

Although the number of reported incapacitation accidents is small, the consequences can be catastrophic. The Safety Board considers alerter systems to be a promising safety improvement and concludes that wheelhouse alerter systems may provide an effective means of preventing operator incapacitation and operator fatigue accidents in the future.

The Safety Board is aware of three companies that are, independently of one another, evaluating the effectiveness of these devices. Although the Board recognizes industry's initiative in developing and evaluating these devices, a coordinated effort inclusive of all aspects of the industry would provide the degree of uniformity needed to ensure a comprehensive evaluation. The Coast Guard Research and Development Center

---

[86] The captain told investigators that the last thing he remembered was being abreast of the buoy and lining up for the bridge. At 6.7 miles per hour, the Safety Board estimated the transit time from the buoy to the bridge to be about 4 minutes.

has the technical staff and experience to evaluate these systems. In light of the Coast Guard's responsibility for safety on the navigable waters of the United States, the ongoing safety partnership between the Coast Guard and the towing industry, and the possible safety improvement that these alerter systems offer, the Safety Board believes that the Coast Guard Research and Development Center should evaluate the utility and effectiveness of wheelhouse alerter systems on inland towing vessels for preventing accidents. The Safety Board hopes that the Coast Guard will work with the towing industry in implementing this recommendation.

Safe Transit Procedures

The Safety Board has addressed the issue of safe transit procedures in several past accident investigations. As a result of the 1983 *City of Greenville* and the 1984 *Erin Marie* accidents,[87] the Safety Board made recommendations to USACE regarding navigational guides for mariners navigating the Western Rivers.[88] As a result of the 1993 *Chris* allision with the Judge William Seeber Bridge in New Orleans, the Safety Board recommended that the Coast Guard, in cooperation with USACE, the Board of Commissioners, and bridge owners, review the conditions and practices in the Inner Harbor Navigation Canal, identify hazards to the safe transit of vessels through the canal and lock system, and implement measures to reduce those hazards.[89]

Despite such initiatives, bridge allisions involving towing vessels continue to occur, often with catastrophic consequences. In the past 10 years, 70 people[90] have died in such accidents, all third parties who happened to be crossing the bridge at the time of the accident. The Coast Guard-AWO Work Group reported that 68 percent of bridge allisions were caused by poor operator decision-making. Consequently, remedial action to prevent or to reduce the frequency of bridge allisions involving towboats must focus not only on the physical characteristics of waterways but also on measures to improve the ability of towing vessel operators to make sound decisions.

Current initiatives to address such human performance issues include the Coast Guard-AWO Bridge Allision Work Group's development of navigation "best practices" for transiting bridges vulnerable to allision and the promotion of CEMSs and the CEMS

---

[87] National Transportation Safety Board, *Ramming of the Poplar Street Bridge by the Towboat* M/V City of Greenville *and its Four-Barge Tow, St. Louis, Missouri, April 2, 1983*, Marine Accident Report NTSB/MAR-83/10 (Washington, DC: NTSB, 1983) and *Ramming of the Poplar Street Bridge by the Towboat* M/V Erin Marie *and its Twelve-Barge Tow, St. Louis, Missouri, April 26, 1984*, Marine Accident Report NTSB/MAR-85/02 (Washington, DC: NTSB, 1985).

[88] Safety Recommendations M-83-96 and M-85-26. See appendix C for more information on these and related recommendations.

[89] NTSB/HAR-94/03, Safety Recommendation M-94-10. See appendix C for more information on this and related recommendations.

[90] The Judge Seeber Bridge accident (NTSB/HAR-94/03) resulted in 1 fatality; the Big Bayou Canot Bridge accident (National Transportation Safety Board, *Derailment of AMTRAK Train No. 2 on the CSXT Big Bayou Canot Bridge Near Mobile, Alabama, September 22, 1993*, Railroad-Marine Accident Report NTSB/RAR-94/01 [Washington, DC: NTSB, 1994]) resulted in 47 fatalities; the Port Isabel-Padre Island Bridge accident (NTSB docket number HWY-01-I-H036) resulted in 8 fatalities; and the I-40 bridge accident resulted in 14 fatalities.

demonstration project. The Safety Board commends the AWO and Coast Guard for their efforts to improve operator performance and concludes that the recommendations of the Coast Guard-AWO Bridge Allision Work Group to improve operator performance and lessons learned from the ongoing CEMS demonstration project, when implemented, should both enhance the safety of towing vessel operations and reduce bridge allision accidents.

Bridge Protection

In the 1960s, when the I-40 bridge was designed and built, pier protection was not required by State or Federal design standards or by USACE's permit process. Following completion of the M-KARNS in 1970, commercial vessel traffic began operating near the bridge. During subsequent bridge inspections in 1977 and 1980, ODOT found that the channel piers had experienced superficial damage, indicating that the piers were vulnerable to vessel impact. Consequently, in 1982, the ODOT submitted an application to the Coast Guard requesting permission to install pier protection cells[91] on the north side of the channel piers to address these problems, though no requirement existed to do so. At that time, the bridge community still lacked standards or guidelines for bridge protection, though, by then, the Coast Guard had completed a study[92] on bridge protection, and the 1980 Sunshine Skyway Bridge accident[93] in Florida had heightened awareness of the vulnerability of bridge piers to vessel impact.

Although ODOT installed pier protection cells inside the navigation channel, the I-40 bridge accident occurred outside the navigation channel. Such occurrences demonstrate that most bridges over navigable water can be struck either within or outside the regular navigation channel by barge tows and individual commercial vessels, thus increasing the complexity of bridge protection. Another such accident involved the *Queen Isabella Causeway*,[94] when the *Brown Water V* and tow struck an unprotected pier 175 feet west of the navigation channel. Four additional accidents[95] investigated by the Safety Board involved vessels that rammed approach piers outside the navigation channel, and another involved an allision with a railroad bridge far from the navigation channel.[96]

However, protecting all substructure components of all bridges from vessel impacts would be an enormous task. The vulnerability of a given bridge to vessel impacts depends on the bridge design, location, current conditions, water depth at the bridge support(s), and the width and vertical clearance of the span(s). The I-40 bridge had 12

---

[91] ODOT completed construction of the protection cells in 1984.

[92] U.S. Coast Guard, *The State of the Art of Bridge Protective Systems and Devices*, USCG Contract CG-71955-A (Washington, DC: USCG, November 1978).

[93] NTSB/MAR-81/03.

[94] NTSB docket number HWY-01-I-H036.

[95] USCG/NTSB/MAR-74/04, NTSB/MAR-78/01, NTSB/MAR-81/03, and NTSB/HAR-94/03.

[96] NTSB/RAR-94/01.

piers in the water, and the draft of the empty barges in this accident was 1 foot, making most of the piers accessible and therefore vulnerable to vessel impacts. According to ODOT, in today's dollars, providing protection cells costs about $300,000 per pier in labor and materials. ODOT also noted that installing protection cells at all piers of the I-40 bridge would cost approximately $6.8 million. The I-40 bridge is just one of Oklahoma's 11 highway crossings on the M-KARNS; six of these 11 crossings have parallel bridges, for a total of 17 bridges with 74 piers in the water. To place a protection cell on both the upstream and downstream sides of the piers and one in between each parallel bridge on the M-KARNS alone would require 128 protection cells at a cost of $39.7 million.[97]

The M-KARNS is just one waterway in one State. Nationwide, Coast Guard records show more than 18,000 highway and railroad bridges spanning about 26,000 miles of commercially navigable waterways. The NBI lists 2,844 highway bridges requiring a bridge permit. Many of these bridges have multiple piers that are vulnerable to vessel impact. The Safety Board concludes that because of the cost, replacing or constructing pier protection for each existing bridge pier vulnerable to vessel impact nationwide may not be reasonable.

Bridge engineers have a tool to effectively assess a given bridge's risk (and acceptable risk) for vessel impact. The AASHTO Vessel Collision Guide Specifications provide guidelines for determining a bridge's risk to impact by assessing vessel and vehicle traffic characteristics and the ability of the bridge to withstand the impact. These guidelines have been incorporated in the LRFD bridge standards, which, after 2007, will become the mandatory standards for all new Federal-aid bridge construction. Florida, with many bridges over water, is already using the LRFD standards for new bridge design.

Louisiana, after the 1993 Judge William Seeber Bridge accident,[98] embarked on a program using the AASHTO Vessel Collision Guide Specifications to evaluate existing bridges over navigable water. After the I-40 bridge accident, ODOT hired a consultant to evaluate bridges at 12 river crossings using the AASHTO Vessel Collision Guide Specifications. Although these standards can and are being used to evaluate the vulnerability of existing bridges to vessel impacts and vehicle collisions, they are not mandatory. To adequately protect the motoring public, bridge owners should be required to evaluate an existing bridge's vulnerability to vessel impact.

Demands on the limited funds in the bridge program are many. According to the NBI, the average age of the more than 590,000 bridges in the United States is 40 years. Approximately 28 percent of these structures are considered deficient, but funding is not available for replacement or rehabilitation.[99] The FHWA sufficiency rating system is a method of measuring one bridge's needs against another when qualifying for limited Federal-aid funds. Currently, the relative risk of a bridge to extreme events such as vessel

---

[97] ODOT estimates include $38.4 million for materials and labor and an additional $1.3 million in mobilization costs.

[98] NTSB/HAR-94/03.

[99] Raymond McCormick, "Lengthening the Span of Bridge Service Life," *TR News,* No. 228 (Washington, DC: Transportation Research Board, September-October 2003).

or vehicle impacts; flooding, including scour and debris loading; seismic events; and, more recently, terrorist attacks, is not part of the sufficiency rating formula. Tools to design new bridges and to evaluate existing bridges for protection against these events are available to bridge engineers through scour assessment methods, the debris loading specification,[100] seismic risk methodology, and the Vessel Collision Guide Specifications. Once the relative risks of extreme events are established, this information can be included in a bridge's sufficiency rating and used to prioritize rehabilitation or replacement, balancing the many different needs of State bridge programs, while not ignoring conditions that can lead to catastrophic events.

The Safety Board therefore concludes that including the relative risk of extreme events in bridge sufficiency ratings and in priority for rehabilitation and replacement would help provide a more accurate assessment of a bridge's risk to collapse and loss of life. Therefore, the Safety Board believes that the FHWA should revise its sufficiency rating system, which prioritizes bridges for rehabilitation and replacement, to include the probability of extreme events, such as vessel impact.

The Safety Board has been working since the 1970s to address the vulnerability of bridges to vessel impact. The Safety Board identified bridge vulnerability as a safety issue in its investigation of the 1972 *SS African Neptune* allision with the Sidney Lanier Bridge at Brunswick, Georgia,[101] and in its investigation of the 1977 towboat *Carolyn* and barge allision with the Chesapeake Bay Bridge and Tunnel.[102] The design of bridge protection devices was addressed in the investigations of the 1977 *SS Floridian* allision with the Benjamin Harris Bridge in Hopewell, Virginia,[103] the 1980 *Summit Venture* allision with the Sunshine Skyway Bridge in Tampa Bay, Florida,[104] and the 1996 *Julie N* allision with the Million Dollar Bridge in Portland, Maine.[105] The Safety Board's report on its investigation of the *Mauvilla* allision with the Big Bayou Canot railroad bridge addressed

---

[100] National Research Council, Transportation Research Board, National Cooperative Highway Research Program Report 445, *Debris Forces on Highway Bridges* (Washington, DC: National Academy Press, 2000).

[101] Safety Recommendation H-72-48 in National Transportation Safety Board, SS African Neptune: *Collision With the Sidney Lanier Bridge at Brunswick, Georgia, on November 7, 1972, With Loss of Life*, Marine Accident Report USCG/NTSB/MAR-74/04 (Washington, DC: NTSB, 1974). See appendix C for more information on this and related recommendations.

[102] National Transportation Safety Board, *Tug* Carolyn *and Barge* Weeks No. 254, *Chesapeake Bay Bridge and Tunnel, September 20-21, 1972*, Marine Accident Report NTSB/MAR-74/02 (Washington, DC: NTSB, 1974).

[103] Safety Recommendation H-78-02 in National Transportation Safety Board, *Ramming of the Benjamin Harrison Bridge by the* SS Floridian *Near Hopewell, Virginia, February 24, 1977*, Marine Accident Report NTSB/MAR-78/01 (Washington, DC: NTSB, 1978). See appendix C for more information on this and related recommendations.

[104] NTSB/MAR-81/03, Safety Recommendations M-81-15 and -20. See appendix C for more information on these and related recommendations.

[105] Safety Recommendation M-98-84 in National Transportation Safety Board, *Postaccident Testing for Alcohol and Other Drugs in the Marine Industry and the Ramming of the Portland-South Portland (Million Dollar) Bridge at Portland, Maine, by the Liberian Tankship* Julie N *on September 27, 1996*, Special Investigation Report NTSB/SIR-98/02 (Washington, DC: NTSB 1998). See appendix C for more information on this and related recommendations.

bridge risk assessment.[106] The vulnerability of existing bridges to vessel impact was discussed extensively in the Safety Board's report of the 1993 towboat *Chris* allision with the Judge William Seeber Bridge in New Orleans, Louisiana,[107] which included recommendations to the FHWA and to AASHTO. Recommendation H-94-8 to FHWA was superseded in 1997 (see appendix C); the recommendation to AASHTO was as follows:

H-94-9

In cooperation with the Federal Highway Administration, broaden the application of risk-assessment and management programs to existing highway bridges. Such programs should include, among other things, a formal assessment of the vulnerability of bridges to vessel collision and collapse.

On December 8, 1994, AASHTO responded, noting that this recommendation was under active consideration by the Standing Committee on Highways' Subcommittee on Bridges and Structures and would be discussed in depth at the May 1995 meeting of the subcommittee. In its June 20, 1995, reply, the Safety Board acknowledged the above and classified Safety Recommendation H-94-9 "Open—Acceptable Response."

At a meeting with Safety Board staff on March 30, 2004, AASHTO indicated that it is investigating additional countermeasures as part of its work on the security and vulnerability assessments of the transportation systems. The Water Transportation Committee also discussed this issue with Safety Board staff at its July 2003 meeting and said it will work with the Standing Committee on Highways' Subcommittee on Bridges and Structures on risk assessment issues.

The Safety Board is disappointed that after 10 years AASHTO has not yet addressed the vulnerability of existing bridges to vessel impact and collapse. In a July 20, 2004, letter to AASHTO, the Safety Board indicated Safety Recommendation H-94-9 remains classified "Open—Acceptable Response." However, given that the intent of Safety Recommendation H-94-9 is covered by the recommendation issued in this report to revise the sufficiency rating system, Safety Recommendation H-94-9 is reclassified "Closed—Superseded."

Motorist Warning Systems

Bridge protection is a multitiered process. Available countermeasures range from providing physical protection against vessel impacts (pier strengthening and pier protection) to instituting measures to prevent allisions from occurring (installing aids to navigation and improving operator decision-making). However, when such countermeasures are unavailable, methods that mitigate the loss of life following a vessel impact, such as motorist warning systems, become necessary.

---

[106] NTSB/RAR-94/01, Safety Recommendations I-94-3 and -4. See appendix C for more information on these and related recommendations.

[107] Safety Recommendations H-94-8 and -9. See appendix C for more information on these and related recommendations.

In this accident, 11 vehicles either fell with the collapsed sections of the bridge or drove off the bridge and into the void. The surviving drivers indicated that they could not see the void in the bridge in time to avoid driving into it. The Safety Board examined the available sight distance for both passenger cars and tractor-semitrailers on the east- and westbound approaches to the void in the bridge. The sight distances ranged from 150 to 350 feet; the minimum total stopping distance[108] at 70 mph for passenger cars was 622 feet and for tractor-semitrailers was 726 feet. The minimum total stopping distance for a tractor-semitrailer traveling at 57 mph (self-reported by one driver) was 514 feet. These total stopping distances are greater than the maximum estimated distance of 350 feet for the first point of possible perception, indicating that some drivers involved in this accident did not have sufficient time to stop their vehicles after detecting the collapsed sections of the bridge. In light of the statements of surviving drivers, estimates of the point of first possible perception, and calculations of total stopping distance, the Safety Board concludes that the drivers in this accident did not have adequate time to detect, identify, and respond to the hazard posed by the collapsed sections of the bridge.

An effective motorist warning system, mounted on or near the bridge and capable of alerting motorists to the bridge failure or directing vehicles to stop, might have prevented some of the vehicles, the majority of which were traveling westbound, from driving off the I-40 bridge. The recreational boater who fired the flare pistol said that he saw at least one vehicle fall with the bridge and that his boat then accelerated toward the bridge and reached the area in about 20 seconds. He also stated that he saw two more vehicles drive off the bridge and called 911; after the call, he saw five more vehicles drive off the bridge before shooting the flare. It is difficult to estimate exactly how much time elapsed between the collapse and the time the truck stopped and blocked the westbound approach. Because westbound vehicles, traveling at 57 to 75 mph, could have traversed the 1,500 feet from the east end of the bridge to the void in 13 to 18 seconds, it can be argued that had warning signs been activated within a few seconds, several of the westbound vehicles probably would have had time to react to the warning signs and stop before driving off the bridge.

As stated earlier, it is difficult to estimate exactly how much time elapsed between the collapse and the time the truckdriver saw the flare, stopped, and blocked the westbound approach with his truck. Further, only by coincidence did the recreational boater witness the accident and have the presence of mind to fire a warning flare. The first emergency responder arrived within 8 minutes of notification of the accident, so, certainly, in the absence of a fishing tournament or other witnesses to the bridge collapse, an effective warning system would have stopped additional vehicles from driving off the bridge. Therefore, the Safety Board concludes that an effective motorist warning system on the I-40 bridge might have mitigated the loss of life in this accident.

The Texas Department of Transportation installed such a system after the 2001 Queen Isabella Causeway Bridge accident,[109] in which 10 vehicles either collapsed with the bridge or drove off the void, resulting in 8 fatalities. This early warning collapse

---

[108] Includes perception/reaction and braking distances.

[109] NTSB docket number HWY-01-I-H036.

detection system, which became operational in March 2004, consists of fiber-optic cable, which, if severed, activates flashing lights to warn motorists of danger ahead. As noted earlier, protecting all bridges against all events is not possible. However, in the case of long bridges with many vulnerable piers, such as the Queen Isabella Causeway, or bridges with curvature that results in sight distance limitations, such as the I-40 bridge, it is critical to protect the motoring public by installing automatic bridge failure detection and warning devices.

The Safety Board has addressed the installation of bridge motorist warning systems in previous accident investigations involving the Lake Pontchartrain Causeway, Sunshine Skyway Bridge, and Sidney Lanier Bridge.[110] The Board is aware of at least one discontinuity warning system that has been installed since these accidents, the one on the Sunshine Skyway Bridge in Florida, which FDOT has characterized as being unreliable. The FHWA is working to improve the reliability of such systems, specifically the ability of long-term monitoring instrumentation to withstand the conditions typically found on bridges, through its March 2004 Structural Health Monitoring initiative and through continuing intelligent transportation systems programs. The development of reliable long-term sensing technology is critical in protecting the motoring public, and the Safety Board encourages the FHWA to continue its efforts to provide reliable motorist warning systems.

Once a reliable long-term detection system has been developed, the FHWA should encourage the States to deploy this technology in comprehensive motorist warning systems; such systems could also be used on bridges vulnerable to collapse from other circumstances such as scour, seismic events, and terrorist attack. The Safety Board therefore believes that the FHWA should develop an effective motorist warning system to stop motor vehicle traffic in the event of a partial or total bridge collapse. In addition, the Vessel Collision Guide Specifications describe motorist warning systems and reference the 1983 FHWA technical advisory; however, neither the specifications nor the technical advisory provide guidance on the use of motorist warning systems. Therefore, the Safety Board believes that once an effective motorist warning system has been developed, AASHTO should provide guidance to the States on its use.

---

[110] (a) National Transportation Safety Board, safety recommendation letter to the Greater New Orleans Expressway Commission, January 8, 1975, notation 1423, Safety Recommendation H-74-42; (b) NTSB/MAR-81/03, Safety Recommendations M-81-18 and -19; and (c) USCG/NTSB/MAR-74/04, Safety Recommendation H-72-48. See appendix C for more information on these and related recommendations.

Conclusions

Findings

1. The captain was not impaired due to alcohol or illegal drugs. Further, neither the weather nor the mechanical condition of the towboat nor the captain's qualifications, experience, familiarity with the river, or workload contributed to the accident. Finally, the emergency response was adequate and timely.

2. The captain's incapacitation was probably not a result of his falling asleep.

3. Although the captain's performance may have been subtly impaired by the low level of diphenhydramine in his blood, and he may have been more prone to falling asleep as a result of taking the medication, neither factor was likely to have accounted for his incapacitation.

4. The captain experienced a sudden loss of consciousness, possibly as the result of an abnormal heart rhythm.

5. The captain had no apparent symptoms of clinical significance prior to the accident, and a reasonable clinical evaluation of the captain before the accident was unlikely to have detected the medical conditions that were discovered through postaccident testing.

6. The quick acting fisherman who fired the warning flare to alert motorists on the bridge probably prevented further loss of life.

7. Wheelhouse alerter systems may provide an effective means of preventing operator incapacitation and operator fatigue accidents in the future.

8. The recommendations of the U.S. Coast Guard-American Waterways Operators Bridge Allision Work Group to improve operator performance and lessons learned from the ongoing Crew Endurance Management System demonstration project, when implemented, should both enhance the safety of towing vessel operations and reduce bridge allision accidents.

9. The presence of either another crewmember in the wheelhouse or a wheelhouse alerter system might have resulted in timely action that could have prevented this accident.

10. Because of the cost, replacing or constructing pier protection for each existing bridge pier vulnerable to vessel impact nationwide may not be reasonable.

11. To adequately protect the motoring public, bridge owners should be required to evaluate an existing bridge's vulnerability to vessel impact.

12. Including the relative risk of extreme events in bridge sufficiency ratings and in priority for rehabilitation and replacement would help provide a more accurate assessment of a bridge's risk to collapse and loss of life.

13. The drivers in this accident did not have adequate time to detect, identify, and respond to the hazard posed by the collapsed sections of the bridge.

14. An effective motorist warning system on the Interstate 40 highway bridge might have mitigated the loss of life in this accident.

Probable Cause

The National Transportation Safety Board determines that the probable cause of the *Robert Y. Love's* allision with the Interstate 40 highway bridge and its subsequent collapse was the captain's loss of consciousness, possibly as the result of an unforeseeable abnormal heart rhythm. Contributing to the loss of life was the inability of motorists to detect the collapsed bridge in time to stop their vehicles.

Recommendations

New Recommendations

As a result of this accident, the Safety Board makes the following safety recommendations:

To the U.S. Coast Guard:

Direct the U.S. Coast Guard Research and Development Center to evaluate the utility and effectiveness of wheelhouse alerter systems on inland towing vessels for preventing accidents. (M-04-3)

To the Federal Highway Administration:

Revise your sufficiency rating system, which prioritizes bridges for rehabilitation and replacement, to include the probability of extreme events, such as vessel impact. (H-04-29)

Develop an effective motorist warning system to stop motor vehicle traffic in the event of a partial or total bridge collapse. (H-04-30)

To the American Association of State Highway and Transportation Officials:

Once an effective motorist warning system has been developed, provide guidance to the States on its use. (H-04-31)

Previously Issued Recommendation Classified in This Report

Safety Recommendation H-94-9, previously issued to the American Association of State Highway and Transportation Officials, is reclassified from "Open—Acceptable Response" to "Closed—Superseded" by Safety Recommendation H-04-29.

H-94-9

In cooperation with the Federal Highway Administration, broaden the application of risk-assessment and management programs to existing highway bridges. Such programs should include, among other things, a formal assessment of the vulnerability of bridges to vessel collision and collapse.

BY THE NATIONAL TRANSPORTATION SAFETY BOARD

Appendix A

Investigation and Public Hearing

The National Transportation Safety Board was notified of this accident from media coverage and the National Response Center on Sunday, May 26, 2002. An investigative team was dispatched that included members from the Washington, D.C.; Atlanta, Georgia; Arlington, Texas; and Denver, Colorado, offices.

Parties to the investigation included the Federal Highway Administration, the U.S. Coast Guard, the U.S. Department of Justice, the State of Oklahoma, and Magnolia Marine Transport Company.

The Safety Board investigated the accident under the authority of the Independent Safety Board Act of 1997, according to Safety Board rules. No public hearing was held.

Appendix B

Vessel Impact Force Calculations

Displacement for the barges

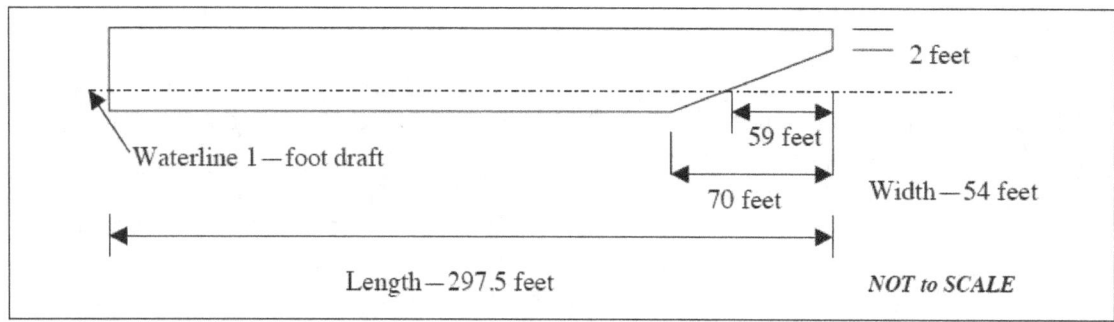

Displacement for *MM-60* (402.6 long tons[1]) + *MM-62* (427.4 long tons) = 830 long tons
830(2,240/2,205) = 843.18 metric tonnes[2]

Displacement calculations for the towboat

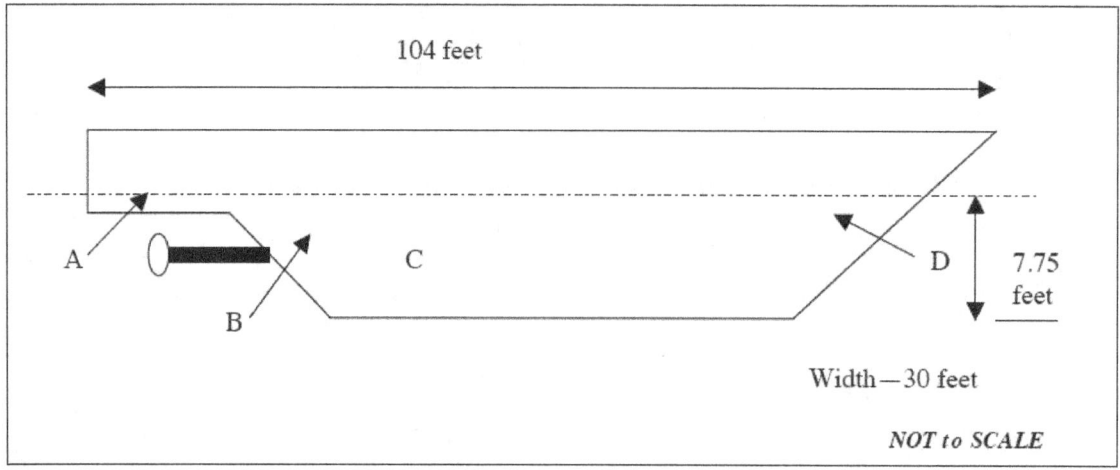

A = (1.75 feet) (38 feet) (30 feet) = 1,995 cf
B = 1/2bh (30) = ½ (25) (6) (30) = 2,250 cf   A+B+C+D = 15,956.25 cf
C = (39) (7.75) (30) = 9,067.50 cf   = 444.50 long tons
D = ½ (7.75) (23.5) (30) = 2,643.75   = 451.56 metric tonnes

---

[1] A long ton equals 2,240 pounds.

[2] A metric tonne equals 2,205 pounds.

Displacement for the tow

Barge 1 + Barge 2 + towboat = 843.18 + 451.56 = 1,294.74 metric tonnes

Kinetic energy of a moving vessel[3]

$$KE = \frac{[C_H \, W \, (V)^2]}{29.2}$$

$C_H = 1.05$ and
$V = 6.7$ mph $= 9.83$ fps
$W =$ displacement tonnage

$$KE = \frac{[(1.05) \, (1,294.74) \, (9.83)^2]}{29.2}$$

$$KE = 4,498.79 \text{ kip-ft}$$

---

[3] American Association of State Highway and Transportation Officials, *Guide Specification and Commentary for Vessel Collision Design of Highway Bridges Volume I: Final Report* (Washington, DC: AASHTO, 1991)16-18.

Appendix C

Previous Recommendations on Safe Transit Procedures, Bridge Vulnerability and Protection, and Motorist Warning Systems

Sidney Lanier Bridge, Brunswick, Georgia—November 7, 1972

The *SS African Neptune* rammed a span adjacent to the draw of the Sidney Lanier Bridge in Brunswick, Georgia, and 450 feet of the bridge collapsed into the Brunswick River.[1] Eight passenger cars and two tractor-semitrailers fell with the bridge, resulting in 10 fatalities and 8 persons hospitalized.

As a result of its investigation of this accident, the Safety Board recommended that the Federal Highway Administration (FHWA), the American Association of State Highway Officials,[2] and the International Bridge, Tunnel and Turnpike Association:

H-72-48

Establish policies and standards to insure that traffic control devices (gate, signals, signs, and pavement markings) are installed on movable bridges at locations which halt traffic on a section of the bridge that is not subject to impact by large marine vessels. Such positioning of warning systems will prevent vehicles from being on those portions of such bridges which may collapse when they are struck by a marine vessel.

On January 1, 1980, the Safety Board classified H-72-48 "Closed—No Longer Applicable."

---

[1] National Transportation Safety Board, SS African Neptune: *Collision With the Sidney Lanier Bridge at Brunswick, Georgia, on November 7, 1972, With Loss of Life*, Marine Accident Report USCG/NTSB/MAR-74/04 (Washington, DC: NTSB, 1974).

[2] The American Association of State Highway Officials (AASHO) became the American Association of State Highway and Transportation Officials (AASHTO) in the 1970s.

Lake Pontchartrain Causeway, New Orleans, Louisiana—August 1, 1974

On August 1, 1974, the towboat, *M/V Miss Andy*, pushing four barges (two abreast), struck the east span of the Lake Pontchartrain Causeway in New Orleans, Louisiana;[3] 252 feet of the bridge collapsed into the water. Two motor vehicles plunged into the lake through the void created by the collapsed deck, resulting in three fatalities. As a result of its investigation of this accident, the Safety Board issued a safety recommendation letter on January 8, 1975, in which it asked the Greater New Orleans Expressway Commission to:

H-74-42

Install a warning system on those sections of the Lake Pontchartrain causeway that are vulnerable to impact by errant marine vessels. The system should activate automatically to warn motorists of danger ahead, should the causeway span collapse.

On January 1, 1980, the Safety Board classified Safety Recommendation H-74-42 "Closed—No Longer Applicable."

Benjamin Harrison Bridge, Hopewell, Virginia—February, 24, 1977

The *SS Marine Floridian*, a bulk sulphur carrier, rammed the support pier between the bridge's northern approach causeway and its northern tower span and continued under the span until the vessel's starboard bridge wing struck the span.[4] The bridge tender was slightly injured while evacuating the bridge; no other injuries occurred. Total property damage was estimated to be $8.5 million.

As a result of its investigation of this accident, the Safety Board recommended that the FHWA:

H-78-2

Work with the U.S. Coast Guard to develop specifications for the design of dolphins, fenders, and other energy absorption and/or vessel redirection devices for the protection of both bridge and vessel during an accidental impact. Issue these design specifications along with guidelines and requirements for the placement of dolphins, fenders and energy absorption and redirection devices.

---

[3] National Transportation Safety Board, safety recommendation letter to the Greater New Orleans Expressway Commission, January 8, 1975, notation 1423.

[4] National Transportation Safety Board, *Ramming of the Benjamin Harrison Bridge by the* SS Floridian *Near Hopewell, Virginia, February 24, 1977*, Marine Accident Report NTSB/MAR-78/01 (Washington, DC: NTSB, 1978).

The FHWA responded that the U.S. Coast Guard (Coast Guard) had sponsored a study on state-of-the-art bridge protective systems and devices and that the FHWA had submitted the specifications developed in this study to AASHTO for consideration as AASHTO specifications. On December 5, 1984, the Safety Board classified Safety Recommendation H-78-2 "Closed—Acceptable Action."

Sunshine Skyway Bridge, Tampa, Florida—May 9, 1980

The Liberian bulk carrier *Summit Venture* rammed a support pier of the western span of the Sunshine Skyway Bridge in Tampa Bay, Florida.[5] The support pier was destroyed and about 1,297 feet of the bridge deck and superstructure fell from a height of about 150 feet into the bay. A Greyhound bus, a small pickup truck, and six automobiles fell into the bay, and 35 persons died. Repair costs were estimated at about $30 million for the bridge and about $1 million for the *Summit Venture*.

As a result of the investigation of this accident, the Safety Board recommended that the Coast Guard:

M-81-15

In cooperation with the Federal Highway Administration, develop standards for the design, performance, and location of structural bridge pier protection systems which consider that the impact from an off-course vessel can occur significantly above as well as below the water surface.

M-81-16

In cooperation with the Federal Highway Administration, conduct a study to determine which existing bridges over the navigable waterways of U.S. ports and harbors are not equipped with adequate structural pier protection.

M-81-17

Distribute a copy of the results of the U.S. Coast Guard's studies regarding bridge and pier protection systems to each appropriate member of the American Association of State Highway and Transportation Officials.

Safety Recommendation M-81-15. On April 13, 1987, the Coast Guard responded that it, in cooperation with the FHWA, had developed a computer program addressing this recommendation and made the program available to AASHTO. On September 4, 1987, the Safety Board classified Safety Recommendation M-81-15 "Closed—Acceptable Action."

Safety Recommendation M-81-16. On September 22, 1981, the Coast Guard responded that it did not concur with this safety recommendation, noting, "We do not have

---

[5] National Transportation Safety Board, *Ramming of the Sunshine Skyway Bridge by the Liberian Bulk Carrier* Summit Venture, *Tampa Bay, Florida, May 9, 1980,* Marine Accident Report NTSB/MAR-81/03 (Washington, DC: NTSB, 1981).

the authority to determine the adequacy of any structural bridge protection system." On May 4, 1982, the Safety Board responded that it could not accept the Coast Guard's reason for not acting on this recommendation. The Board further asked for the Coast Guard's interpretation of Section 101 (7) of the 1972 Ports and Waterways Safety Act, as applicable to the issue of bridge pier protection. The Board also stated, "We do not view the Coast Guard's role as administrator of the Ports and Waterways Safety Act and the Federal bridge permit program as [limiting] highway bridge protection measures to those involving vessel operations." On April 13, 1987, the Coast Guard responded:

> The Coast Guard does not concur with this recommendation. As we stated in our previous response to this recommendation, we do not have the authority to determine the adequacy of any structural bridge protection system. Therefore, no further action on this recommendation is anticipated.

Consequently, on February 17, 1987, the Safety Board classified Safety Recommendation M-81-16 "Open—Unacceptable Action." The Safety Board later reclassified Safety Recommendation M-81-16 "Closed—Unacceptable Action" as a result of its investigation of a 1987 allision involving the Sidney Lanier Bridge.[6]

Safety Recommendation M-81-17. On April 13, 1987, the Coast Guard indicated that criteria for the design of bridge piers to withstand vessel impacts had been sent to AASHTO. The Coast Guard also noted that the FHWA had prepared and distributed a technical advisory on this subject. On September 4, 1987, the Safety Board classified Safety Recommendation M-81-17 "Closed—Acceptable Action."

Also as a result of its investigation of the accident involving the Sunshine Skyway Bridge,[7] the Safety Board recommended that the FHWA:

M-81-18

Develop standards for the design, performance, and installation of bridge span failure detection and warning systems.

M-81-19

Establish criteria to evaluate the need for installing bridge span failure detection and warning systems on existing and proposed bridges.

M-81-20

In cooperation with the U.S. Coast Guard, develop standards for the design, performance, and location of structural bridge pier protection systems which consider that the impact from an off-course vessel can occur significantly above as well as below the water surface.

---

[6] National Transportation Safety Board, *Ramming of the Sidney Lanier Bridge by the Polish Bulk Carrier* Ziemia Bialostocka, *Brunswick, Georgia, May 3, 1987*, Marine Accident Report NTSB/MAR-88/03 (Washington, DC: NTSB, 1988).

[7] NTSB/MAR-81/03.

M-81-21

In cooperation with the U.S. Coast Guard, conduct a study to determine which existing bridges over the navigable waterways of U.S. ports and harbors are not equipped with adequate structural pier protection.

M-81-22

Use the results of the study conducted under Safety Recommendation M-81-21 to advise appropriate bridge authorities of the benefits of installing additional pier protection systems.

Safety Recommendation M-81-18. The FHWA's responses on August 14, 1981, and February 25, 1983, indicated that the FHWA sent a memorandum to the field offices stating that the most practical existing span failure warning system is an electrical conductor system attached to the bridge that activates warning systems when its continuity is disrupted by span failure or collapse. In addition, the FHWA developed a technical advisory, "Pier Protection and Warning Systems for Bridges Subject to Ship Collisions," dated February 11, 1983, providing information on the advantages and disadvantages of alternate types of warning systems, the design of bridge span detection warning systems, and the warrants for the need for such systems on Federal-aid highway projects. On May 4, 1983, the Safety Board classified Safety Recommendation M-81-18 "Closed—Acceptable Action."

Safety Recommendation M-81-19. The FHWA's responses on August 14, 1981, and February 25, 1983, indicated that the FHWA had provided guidance for warrants for open-span failure warning systems in a December 8, 1980, memorandum to FHWA regional administrators, "Motorist Warning Systems on Bridges Subject to Ship Collisions." The memorandum stated that decisions to install such systems should be based upon: (1) the type and frequency of shipping on the waterways; (2) the location and arrangement of the bridge piers in relation to the navigable channel and the resulting vulnerability of the piers to vessel impacts; (3) other factors (such as fog, channel geometrics, wind, and river currents) that may create navigational problems in the vicinity of the bridge; and (4) the volume of highway traffic using the bridge. The FHWA further stated that these warrants were also included in the February 11, 1983, technical advisory, as noted in its response to Safety Recommendation M-81-18. On May 4, 1983, the Safety Board classified Safety Recommendation M-81-19 "Closed—Acceptable Action."

Safety Recommendation M-81-20. On March 5, 1984, the FHWA indicated that because of the low probability of vessel-bridge impacts, the extraordinary costs required to design bridge piers to withstand the impact of large ships, and the limited funds available to carry out the national bridge program, it and the Coast Guard had agreed rather than to design all water piers in navigable waters to withstand the full impact loads of modern vessels, they would instead evaluate each bridge crossing on a case-by-case basis to determine the degree of pier protection necessary. The FHWA noted that the following guidance has been made available for this evaluation:

- Standards for pier protection systems that are being evaluated by an AASHTO task force; and

- A report containing information on bridge pier design prepared by the Marine Board of the National Research Council *(Ship Collisions With Bridges)* and distributed to all FHWA field offices and State highway agencies through a memorandum on November 30, 1983. This memorandum requests that field offices fully address the potential problems of vessel-bridge impacts in ongoing Federal-aid projects through the Coast Guard/FHWA coordination procedures associated with Coast Guard bridge permits for navigable water crossings. The FHWA further stated that the Marine Board report noted above discusses the fact that the impact of an off-course vessel can occur significantly above, as well as below, the water line.

On December 5, 1984, the Safety Board classified Safety Recommendation M-81-20 "Closed—Acceptable Action."

Safety Recommendation M-81-21. On March 5, 1984, the FHWA responded that, as noted in its response to Safety Recommendation M-81-20, pier protection evaluations must be made on a case-by-case basis. The FHWA also stated that it had anticipated that the November 1983 study, *Ship Collisions With Bridges*, mentioned in its response to Safety Recommendation M-81-20, would address this safety recommendation but that this report did not specifically identify existing bridges in navigable waters with inadequate structural pier protection.

The FHWA further responded that it did not have the resources to conduct the requested study; it noted, however, that all highway bridges, including bridge piers and fendering systems, were being inspected on a regular basis by their respective State and local highway agencies. On October 30, 1984, the FHWA issued a memorandum to field offices instructing them to ensure that State inspections of bridges over navigable waters continued to include an assessment and evaluation of bridge piers and fendering systems for structural integrity, as provided for in the *Bridge Inspector's Training Manual*.

On April 19, 1985, the Safety Board requested additional information from the FHWA regarding: (1) inspection criteria to be used by State highway bridge inspectors, (2) qualifications of State inspectors, and (3) methods to be used by State inspectors to evaluate pier protection overall. On July 16, 1985, the FHWA replied:

In response to Item 1, as noted in earlier responses, there is no universal standard which can be developed to determine whether a given pier protection system is needed or whether an existing one is adequate. Such determination must be made on a case-by-case basis considering the waterway usage. However, general criteria and procedures can be developed and then modified for individual State requirements. These criteria should be developed where appropriate by the individual in charge of the State's bridge inspection program in conjunction with those responsible for pier protection design.

The bridge inspector, through site inspections, can identify and provide information on the type, size, location and condition of pier protection systems. However, in many instances, he will not have sufficient data, training, or experience to evaluate the adequacy of the system. A judgment as to adequacy of a system should more appropriately be made by the State bridge engineer, through an evaluation of the inspection data, in conjunction with other available information.

A publication listing all bridges over the navigable waters of the United States is available to the States. This listing identifies those bridges where pier protection systems must at least be considered.

The State of Louisiana has developed a manual titled *Criteria For: The Design of Bridge Piers with respect to Vessel Collision in Louisiana Waterways*. Although specifically prepared for Louisiana, the manual provides in-depth procedures for analyzing and designing bridges to minimize vessel collisions. This manual has been distributed to all States through the AASHTO Highway Subcommittee on Bridges and Structures and was discussed at the national meetings held in 1985. The manual was referred back to the subcommittee for further review and development for consideration and later adoption as national standards.

In response to Item 2, the National Bridge Inspection Standards (NBIS) are very specific on bridge inspector qualifications. The requirements of a graduate engineer or a combination of experience and training assure that qualified inspectors will obtain accurate information on the type, size, location, and condition of any existing pier protection system.

In response to Item 3, the information provided by the bridge inspector will be used with other available information on the stream characteristics, location of channel piers, type and volume of river traffic, etc., to analyze each site for required pier protection. Engineering judgment must be used in assessing the risk versus the consequences of bridge pier collisions along with the cost effectiveness in the development of possible pier protection systems.

In summary, the qualified bridge inspector will provide the needed site-specific information. This inspection data will be used with other available State criteria, or with criteria developed by others, to analyze and develop any needed pier protection systems. Even though national standards have not yet been adopted, they are under development through the appropriate AASHTO committee. The Louisiana criteria provided to each State could serve as an interim guide pending further development of national criteria.

On November 19, 1985, the Safety Board classified Safety Recommendation M-81-21 "Closed—Acceptable Alternate Action."

Safety Recommendation M-81-22. On March 4, 1984, the FHWA responded that it would continue to assess the integrity of pier protection systems through the national bridge inspection program. According to the FHWA, the results of each bridge inspection were provided to the appropriate bridge authorities for their review and subsequent action to correct identified deficiencies, and the inspection and review of bridge piers and fender systems through the national bridge inspection program would accomplish an ongoing review of the structural integrity of existing pier protective systems. The FHWA also stated that as additional technical information became available concerning the evaluation of pier protection systems on existing bridges, it would include it to the extent practicable in the ongoing national bridge inspection program.

The FHWA also noted that Federal-aid highway funds could be used to cover the costs of warranted warning and pier protection systems for bridges on all public highways, if such costs were associated with bridge projects funded under the Highway Bridge Replacement and Rehabilitation Program. On April 19, 1985, the Safety Board classified Safety Recommendation M-81-22 "Closed—Acceptable Alternate Action."

Poplar Street Bridge, St. Louis, Missouri—April 2, 1983

The towboat *City of Greenville,* pushing four barges laden with crude oil, struck a pier of the Poplar Street Bridge, which crosses the Upper Mississippi River between St. Louis, Missouri, and East St. Louis, Illinois.[8] At least one barge was ruptured by the impact, and crude oil was released and ignited almost immediately. Three barges broke loose and floated downriver. One barge sank about a mile from the bridge, a second barge collided with barges moored at a chemical barge loading facility, and the other barge collided with a grain barge loading terminal. The facilities sustained severe damage. The burning oil ignited several fires along about 2 miles of waterfront on the Illinois side of the river and polluted approximately 10 miles of the river. One person was injured as a result of this accident. The damage to the barge loading facilities, the grain barges, and their cargos; the damage and loss of cargo to the tow of the *City of Greenville*; and the cost of the oil cleanup operations were estimated to be about $9 million. As a result of its investigation of this accident, the Safety Board recommended that the U.S. Army Corps of Engineers (USACE):

M-83-96

Develop and publish a navigation guide or guides for mariners navigating the Western Rivers similar in format to the *United States Coast Pilot*.

---

[8] National Transportation Safety Board, *Ramming of the Poplar Street Bridge by the Towboat* M/V City of Greenville *and its Four-Barge Tow, St. Louis, Missouri, April 2, 1983*, Marine Accident Report NTSB/MAR-83/10 (Washington, DC: NTSB, 1983).

On June 29, 1984, USACE responded, "[T]he primary responsibility for safe navigation on the inland waterways lies with towboat pilots, who in addition to being experienced and well-trained need to have a through knowledge of the waterway being traveled." While it agreed such a publication could be a useful tool, USACE stated that it did not believe that publishing such a guide was appropriate, since publishing was not a logical extension of USACE's duties. USACE indicated it would continue the practice of advising mariners, through local notices to navigation interests, of conditions on the rivers that could affect navigation, such as shoaling, river stages, and outdraft conditions at locks. On June 26, 1985, the Safety Board classified Safety Recommendation M-83-96 "Closed—Reconsidered."

Poplar Street Bridge, St. Louis, Missouri—April 26, 1984

The towboat *Erin Marie,* pushing 12 barges laden with grain downriver in high water conditions, struck a pier of the Poplar Street Bridge, which crosses the Upper Mississippi River between St. Louis, Missouri, and East St. Louis, Illinois.[9] Several barges broke free and floated downriver, striking a fleet of 23 barges, breaking them free from their moorings, and causing them to float free downriver. The barges in turn struck other fleeted barges and shoreside facilities. More than 150 barges and vessels were broken free of their moorings and cast adrift in the river. The total damages to barges, cargo, fleeting areas, and barge loading facilities was estimated at $3 million. No one was injured. As a result of its investigation, the Safety Board recommended that USACE:

M-85-26

In the next edition of the Upper Mississippi River Navigation Charts, provide supplemental large scale charts for harbor areas, and areas difficult to navigate due to current conditions, sharp bends, or restricted navigation clearances; and areas having a higher-than-average accident rate or where there are recurrent major accidents. Incorporate on all charts the location of fleeting areas and other important waterside features.

On December 30, 1992, USACE replied that it:

(1) prepares notices to navigation interests and regularly coordinates with the Coast Guard on unusual channel conditions, (2) identifies important waterside features (including fleeting areas) on its navigation charts, [and that] (3) barge fleeting areas and harbor features are presented in map and tabular form, and (4) bridge configurations are shown in profile with dimensions and clearances. However, large-scale maps for harbor areas are not provided.

On March 4, 1993, the Safety Board acknowledged that USACE provides mariners with all of the requested information except for large-scale maps of harbor areas and classified Safety Recommendation M-85-26 "Closed—Acceptable Alternate Action."

---

[9] National Transportation Safety Board, *Ramming of the Poplar Street Bridge by the Towboat* M/V Erin Marie *and its Twelve-Barge Tow, St. Louis, Missouri, April 26, 1984*, Marine Accident Report NTSB/MAR-85/02 (Washington, DC: NTSB, 1985).

Sidney Lanier Bridge in Brunswick, Georgia—May 3, 1987

On May 3, 1987, the Polish Bulk carrier *Ziemia Bialostocka* rammed the Sidney Lanier Bridge,[10] resulting in about $1.4 million in damage to the bridge and causing a 4-month bridge closure at an additional estimated cost of $7.9 million. As a result of its investigation, the Safety Board recommended that the State of Georgia:

M-88-25

Modify the fenders on the Sidney Lanier Bridge to protect the bridge from minor impact of large vessels.

M-88-26

Review the fenders on other Georgia bridges and modify the fenders to protect bridges from minor impacts of large vessels.

Safety Recommendation M-88-25. On January 18, 1989, the State of Georgia indicated that a study was underway to determine whether the Sidney Lanier Bridge should be replaced and noted that the damaged fendering system had been repaired. On March 23, 1989, the Safety Board classified Safety Recommendation M-88-25 "Open—Acceptable Response." On May 20, 1993, the State of Georgia indicated, based upon its study and Coast Guard analysis, that Congress had designated the Sidney Lanier Bridge an "obstruction to navigation"[11] and committed to a 50-percent share in the replacement of the bridge. On July 20, 1993, the Safety Board noted that it was pleased work had begun on a replacement for the Sidney Lanier Bridge and that the new bridge design would incorporate "island" bridge protection. Accordingly, Safety Recommendation M-88-25 was classified "Closed—Acceptable Action."

Safety Recommendation M-88-26. On January 18, 1989, the State of Georgia indicated that only two of its bridges (the Sidney Lanier Bridge in Brunswick and the Talmadge Bridge in Savannah) had a potential for impact by oceangoing vessels. The State of Georgia further noted that the new Sidney Lanier Bridge would have "island" bridge protection and that none of the new Talmadge Bridge's supporting substructures would be in water deep enough to support oceangoing vessels. On March 21, 1989, the Safety Board classified Safety Recommendation M-88-26 "Closed—Acceptable Action."

---

[10] NTSB/MAR-88/03.

[11] A requirement for eligibility for funding under the The Act of June 21, 1940, as amended (Truman-Hobbs Act), (54 Stat. 497; 33 U.S.C. 511-523).

Judge William Seeber Bridge, New Orleans, Louisiana—May 28, 1993

The towboat *Chris*, pushing the empty hopper barge *DM 3021*, collided with a support pier of the eastern span of the Judge William Seeber Bridge over the Industrial Canal in New Orleans.[12] The impact severed bent 21, causing two approach spans and the two-column bent to collapse onto the barge and into the shallow waters of the canal. Two automobiles carrying three people fell with the four-lane bridge deck, resulting in one death and serious injuries to two persons. As a result of this accident, the canal was closed to navigation traffic for 2 days, and the bridge was closed to vehicular traffic for 2 months. The accident resulted in approximately $2 million in damage to the bridge and $7,000 in damage to barge *DM 3021*. As a result of its investigation of this accident, the Safety Board recommended that the FHWA:

H-94-8

In cooperation with the American Association of State Highway Transportation Officials, broaden the application of risk-assessment and management programs to existing highway bridges. Such programs should include, among other things, a formal assessment of the vulnerability of bridges to vessel collision and collapse.

On March 27, 1997, the FHWA suggested that Safety Recommendation H-94-8 had been superseded by Safety Recommendations I-94-3 and -4 (from the 1993 Bayou Canot Railroad Bridge accident). On October 7, 1997, the Safety Board agreed with the FHWA and classified Safety Recommendation H-94-8 "Closed—No Longer Applicable/Superseded."

Also as result of this investigation, the Safety Board recommended that AASHTO:

H-94-9

In cooperation with the Federal Highway Administration, broaden the application of risk-assessment and management programs to existing highway bridges. Such programs should include, among other things, a formal assessment of the vulnerability of bridges to vessel collision and collapse.

On December 8, 1994, AASHTO responded, noting that this recommendation was under active consideration by the Standing Committee on Highways' Subcommittee on Bridges and Structures and would be discussed in depth at the May 1995 meeting of the subcommittee. In its June 20, 1995, reply, the Safety Board acknowledged the above reply and classified Safety Recommendation H-94-9 "Open—Acceptable Response."

At a meeting with Safety Board staff on March 30, 2004, AASHTO indicated that it is investigating additional countermeasures as part of its work on the security and

---

[12] National Transportation Safety Board, *U. S. Towboat* Chris *Collision With the Judge William Seeber Bridge New Orleans, Louisiana, May 28, 1993,* Highway-Marine Accident Report NTSB/HAR-94/03 (Washington, DC: NTSB, 1994).

vulnerability assessments of the transportation systems. The Water Transportation Committee also discussed this issue with Safety Board staff at its July 2003 meeting and said it will work with the Standing Committee on Highways' Subcommittee on Bridges and Structures on risk-assessment issues.

In a July 20, 2004, letter to AASHTO, the Safety Board indicated Safety Recommendation H-94-9 remains classified "Open—Acceptable Response." However, given that the intent of Safety Recommendation H-94-9 is covered by the recommendation issued in this report to revise the sufficiency rating system, Safety Recommendation H-94-9 is reclassified "Closed—Superseded."

Also as a result of its investigation of the accident involving the Judge William Seeber bridge, the Safety Board recommended that the Coast Guard:

<u>M-94-10</u>

Coordinate a cooperative effort with the United States Army Corps of Engineers, the Board of Commissioners of the Port of New Orleans, and bridge owners to review conditions and practices in the Inner Harbor Navigation Canal, identify hazards to the safe transit of vessels through the canal and lock system, and implement measures to reduce those hazards.

In correspondence dated February 14, 1995, and September 23, 1996, the Coast Guard indicated that it had been working with USACE and the city of New Orleans. The Coast Guard also stated that during the repair of the Judge William Seeber Bridge, pier protection had been installed and that pier protection was planned for the Florida Avenue Bridge.

On March 20, 1997, the Safety Board noted that it had learned USACE was planning a new lock in the industrial canal that should eliminate many of the problems associated with the existing lock. The Board further noted that it believed the construction of a larger lock would attract larger tows and not necessarily reduce the hazards associated with the existing lock and asked the Coast Guard how it would address the last part of Safety Recommendation M-94-10, requesting that it identify hazards to the safe transit of vessels through the canal and lock system and implement measures to reduce those hazards.

On April 3, 2001, the Coast Guard responded that USACE had a lock replacement and Inner Navigation Canal Improvement project underway that would necessitate modification of the Claiborne Avenue Bridge (Judge William Seeber Bridge) and replacement of the Claude Avenue Bridge. The Coast Guard further stated that a Truman-Hobbs Act rehabilitation/alteration project was in progress on the Florida Avenue Bridge. The Coast Guard noted that these improvement projects were based on the results of a national bridge survey completed in 1996. The Coast Guard also stated that the bridges over the waterway had sufficient clearances and pier protection to meet the reasonable needs of land and water traffic without undue hazards and stated that it found no compelling need to implement additional measures to ensure the safe transit of vessels through the canal and lock system.

In its reply, the Safety Board acknowledged that the Coast Guard had provided information regarding actions that it had taken to improve the safety of navigation in the canal, had studied the hazard conditions in the canal, and had taken what it believed to be appropriate action to mitigate those hazards. Accordingly, on February 2, 2002, the Safety Board classified Safety Recommendation M-94-10 "Closed—Acceptable Action."

Big Bayou Canot Railroad Bridge Near Mobile, Alabama—September 22, 1993

About 2:45 a.m., the towboat *Mauvilla,* pushing six barges, struck and displaced the Big Bayou Canot railroad bridge near Mobile, Alabama.[13] Eight minutes later, AMTRAK train 2, the Sunset Limited, en route from Los Angeles, California, to Miami, Florida, with 220 persons on board, struck the displaced bridge and derailed. The three locomotive units, the baggage and dormitory cars, and two of the six passenger cars fell into the water. The fuel tanks on the locomotive units ruptured, and the locomotive units and the baggage and dormitory cars caught fire. Forty-two passengers and 5 crewmembers were killed; 103 passengers were injured. The towboat's four crewmembers were not injured. As a result of its investigation of this accident, the Safety Board recommended that the U.S. Department of Transportation (DOT):

I-94-3

Convene an intermodal task force that includes the Coast Guard, the Federal Railroad Administration, the Federal Highway Administration, and the U.S. Army Corps of Engineers to develop a standard methodology for determining the vulnerability of the Nation's highway and railroad bridges to collisions from marine vessels, to formulate a ranking system for identifying bridges at greatest risk, and to provide guidance on the effectiveness and appropriateness of protective measures.

I-94-4

Require that the Federal Railroad Administration and the Federal Highway Administration, for their respective modes, use the methodology developed by the intermodal task force to carry out a national risk-assessment program for the Nation's railroad and highway bridges.

On April 24, 1997, the DOT responded that an intermodal task force had completed a screening of bridges across navigable waters that are particularly vulnerable to damage by commercial marine traffic. The DOT further stated that the task force used 10 major risk factors in determining which bridges may need new or enhanced bridge fendering and lighting systems and that the task force, especially the Federal Railroad Administration, relied upon the Coast Guard's screening and evaluation to prioritize improvements for navigation at the bridge sites.

---

[13] National Transportation Safety Board, *Derailment of AMTRAK Train No. 2 on the CSXT Big Bayou Canot Bridge Near Mobile, Alabama, September 22, 1993,* Railroad-Marine Accident Report NTSB/RAR-94/01 (Washington, DC: NTSB, 1994).

The Safety Board replied that although the methods used and the program established by the intermodal task force were less vigorous than the Safety Board expected, the program would reduce the risk of marine vessel impacts with bridges over navigable waters. Consequently, on October 27, 1998, the Safety Board classified Safety Recommendations I-94-3 and -4 "Closed—Acceptable Alternate Action."

Million Dollar Bridge, Portland, Maine—September 27, 1996

The 540-foot-long Liberian tankship *Julie N,* carrying a cargo of heating oil, collided with the south bascule pier of the Portland-South Portland Million Dollar Bridge.[14] Although no injuries occurred, the accident resulted in a 33-foot-long hole in the vessel's hull beneath the waterline. About 4,000 barrels of oil spilled into the harbor. The vessel sustained about $660,000 in damage, and the cost for cleanup of the oil was approximately $43 million. Repairs to the bridge were about $232,000. As a result of its investigation of this accident, the Safety Board recommended that the FHWA:

M-98-83

Inform State highway departments of the circumstances of the accident and recommend that the States evaluate the adequacy of fendering systems at bridge piers where the systems were not designed for the type and size of vessel currently using the waterway and may not be adequate to protect the bridge and take corrective action as necessary.

On August 27, 1998, the FHWA responded that it would inform State transportation departments of the circumstances of the Million Dollar Bridge accident and reinforce its previous guidance to the States regarding this matter. On October 21, 1998, the Safety Board acknowledged that the FHWA had issued a memorandum to the FHWA field offices recommending that the States evaluate the adequacy of fendering systems at bridge piers where the systems were not designed for the type and size of vessels currently using the waterway and take corrective action, as necessary, in accordance with their overall, ongoing Bridge Management System Programs, and consequently classified Safety Recommendation M-98-03 "Closed—Acceptable Action."

---

[14] National Transportation Safety Board, *Postaccident Testing for Alcohol and Other Drugs in the Marine Industry and the Ramming of the Portland-South Portland (Million Dollar) Bridge at Portland, Maine, by the Liberian Tankship* Julie N *on September 27, 1996,* Special Investigation Report NTSB/SIR-98/02 (Washington, DC: NTSB, 1998).

Also as a result of its investigation, the Safety Board recommended that AASHTO:

<u>M-98-84</u>

Inform State highway departments of the circumstances of the accident and recommend that the States evaluate the adequacy of fendering systems at bridge piers where the systems were not designed for the type and size of vessel currently using the waterway and may not be adequate to protect the bridge and take corrective action as necessary.

On April 17, 2000, AASHTO responded that the FHWA memorandum had been distributed to the AASHTO Standing Committee on Highways' Subcommittee on Bridges and Structures (consisting of State bridge engineers) and had been discussed at its May 1999 meeting. On June 27, 2000, the Safety Board classified Safety Recommendation M-98-84 "Closed—Acceptable Action."

www.ingramcontent.com/pod-product-compliance
Lightning Source LLC
Chambersburg PA
CBHW081132290526
45795CB00006B/2204